GREAT GOLF HUMOR
FROM GOLF DIGEST

Edited by Larry Sheehan

A Golf Digest Book

ACKNOWLEDGMENTS

"The Coming of Gowf" from "The Golf Omnibus" by P. G.
Wodehouse, copyright © 1973 by P. G. Wodehouse. Reprinted
by permission of Simon and Schuster, a division of Gulf &
Western Corporation.

"Golf Is a Trip" from "Picked-Up Pieces," by John Updike,
copyright © 1973 by John Updike. Reprinted by permission of
Alfred A. Knopf, Inc.

"The Halter-Top Capital of the Tournament World"
(original title "The Greening of Cowtown"), copyright © 1977
by Texas Monthly. Reprinted with permission from the
August 1977 issue of Texas Monthly.

"How I Hustled $180,000 in a Week of Golf" from
"Court Hustler" by Bobby Riggs and George McGann (J. B.
Lippincott Company). Copyright © 1973 by Robert L. Riggs
and George McGann. Reprinted by permission of Harper &
Row, Publishers, Inc.

Published by Golf Digest, Inc.
A New York Times Company
495 Westport Avenue
Norwalk, Connecticut 06856

Trade book distribution by
Simon and Schuster
A Division of Gulf & Western
    Corporation
New York, New York 10020

First Printing
ISBN: 0-914178-31-8
Library of Congress: 79-52547
Manufactured in the
    United States of America

EDITOR'S NOTE

During the past three decades, a wide range of lighthearted writing has found its way into the pages of Golf Digest: witty essays, spoofs and parodies, fables, madcap travelogs, first-person accounts of shanking or yipping or slicing. All these forms, and others, were written by a varied and distinguished array of authors—Norman Cousins, John Updike, P. G. Wodehouse, Dan Jenkins—to name a few.

In this volume, "Great Golf Humor," we have tried to retain the same eclectic nature and variety, so we have reason to hope that all golfers will find much here to please them.

For reviewing my preliminary selections and making valuable suggestions, I would like to thank Golf Digest associate publisher Paul Menneg, editor Nick Seitz and managing editor Jay Simon.

—Larry Sheehan, Editor

ABOUT THE CONTRIBUTORS

FRANK BOGGS is the sports editor and columnist for the Oklahoma City Times.

CHARLES BROME is managing editor of Golf Journal, the publication of the United States Golf Association (USGA).

GARY CARTWRIGHT was golf editor at the Dallas Morning News before moving to Austin, where he is now a free-lance writer.

JAY CRONLEY's humor has appeared in newspapers and magazines. He has written two novels.

JOSEPH C. DEY is the former USGA executive director and PGA Commissioner.

PETER DOBEREINER, who writes a regular column for Golf Digest, is golf correspondent for the London Observer.

WILLIAM PRICE FOX is writer-in-residence at the University of South Carolina and author of several novels plus the humorous "Doctor Golf."

DAN GLEASON is a free-lance writer, whose book about the pro tour, "The Great, The Grand, and the Also-Ran," appeared in 1976.

DAN JENKINS, senior writer at Sports Illustrated, wrote the best-selling books, "Semi-Tough" and "Dead Solid Perfect."

HENRY LONGHURST was a Golf Digest columnist prior to his death in 1978. For many years, he was the golf correspondent of the London Sunday Times and a commentator of U.S. golf telecasts, notably the Masters.

JIM MURRAY's daily column for the Los Angeles Times is syndicated nationally.

BRENNAN QUINN is a free-lance writer who lives in California.

BOBBY RIGGS ranked near the top of the world's tennis players during the 1940's.

NICK SEITZ is the editor of Golf Digest and has written "Superstars of Golf" and co-authored "Teed Off" with outspoken touring professional, Dave Hill.

LARRY SHEEHAN is a contributing editor of Golf Digest who has written several sports books, among them "The New Golf Mind" with Gary Wiren and Richard Coop and "You Can Hit the Golf Ball Farther" with Evan Williams.

K. JASON SITEWELL is the golfing alias of long-time Saturday Review editor Norman Cousins.

JOHN UPDIKE is one of America's most esteemed novelists, whose works include the popular "Couples," "Rabbit Run" and "Rabbit Redux."

P. G. WODEHOUSE wrote numerous wacky stories about golf as well as a prodigious number of novels.

CARTOONISTS whose works appear in this book: Richard Andrew, Herb Brammeier, Dave Gerard, David Harbaugh, Reg Hider, John Jonik, Jeff Keate, Dick Kenehan, Edwin Lepper, Bill Maul, Clem Scalzitti and W. A. Vanselow.

"Hold it. Your stance is **all** wrong."

CONTENTS

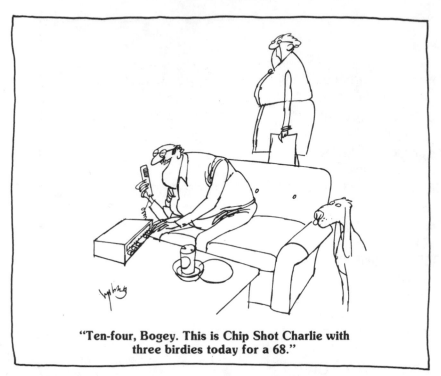

"Ten-four, Bogey. This is Chip Shot Charlie with three birdies today for a 68."

"Sorry. You've crossed the forbidden boundary of the Woodchkins."

WANT TO HIT IT 553 YARDS? SEND MONEY.

by PETER DOBEREINER

On my home course, we have a killer hole about 460 yards and sharply doglegged to the right around a stand of noble beech trees. The other day I was going through my regular routine in preparation to tackle the monster. This involves sucking in six deep breaths to load the system with oxygen, plus a mental windup based on yoga, self-hypnosis and a Zen exercise designed to persuade me that, sure, I can hit a power fade around the corner. Just as I was about to unleash my double-hernia swing, a companion remarked, "Remember how you always used to whip one straight over those trees with your 4-wood?"

It was a cruel reminder of my advancing years. My game plan— to follow the drive with a blue-flamer fairway wood, then a middle iron and hope to chip in for my par—was shattered. That evening I slumped into a chair, tucked a vitamin tablet under my tongue and sought solace from numerous back issues of renowned golf magazines from around the world. Since I had already read the articles, I concentrated on the advertisements and gradually my spirits revived. Gad, what a fool I had been. Here, under my very nose, lay the answer to declining physical powers.

A pair of socks with a miracle sole, guaranteed to add 10 yards to my drive. Shoes promising another 10 yards, thanks to a similar miracle of technology and long-lasting tungsten spikes to boot. What's a few measly bucks? I'd give my entire fortune, which consists of a few measly bucks, incidentally, for an extra 20 yards.

That dream proved to be mere chicken feed. Now came the real stuff. A fancy grip promised to release the tremendous power in my legs and drive the ball 300 yards or more. And only $6.95. Next comes a driver with an aerodynamic design to give me an extra 10 yards. If I get one of those and fit it with a graphite shaft (guaranteed 10 percent more distance) and my new grip, that is 300 yards plus 10 plus 10 percent. Wow, 341 yards!

For a mere $1.75 I can get a repair manual which will show me how to assemble this wonder club. Add my extra 20 yards for shoes and socks and I am up to 361 yards. That is before I have

11

even pulled on a glove. What latent power lies in gloves. I never dreamed that a glove could make me hit a ball 10 yards farther, but here they are, complete with guarantee. Now, 371 yards.

Frankly, I am not overimpressed by the promises of swing trainers, practice nets, standing on a mat marked with Sam Snead's footprints, muscle builders and fast improvement plans, "guaranteed to take five to 15 strokes off your scores."

The same goes for range finders which will save me five strokes a round or a book of putting hints which will produce instant rhythm, tempo and overspin for $18.95 and save me another seven to 15 strokes a round. Right now I am into power and I do not particularly want to take advantage of the promised 40 strokes which I could save every round by using all these aids, some of them not legal. I would make Jack Nicklaus look a fool, and I have no wish to do that. I just want to outdrive him.

Here is a device which looks like an ankle shackle from the chain-gang days. It will stop my swaying and enable me to hit the ball farther, harder and straighter, a bargain at $14.95 even if the extra distance is not actually specified. And what of this loaded wrist strap whose "miracle motion of weights develops real club-head speed?" I will take a chance and accept the offer to rush me one for only $4.95, although I am worried about using it in conjunction with my wonder glove. Perhaps I could wear it on my other ankle to help release that tremendous power in my legs.

Between the two of them I should get an extra 10 yards at least. So far, all my calculations have been based on a regular golf ball and that has clearly been a mistake, for here we have an announcement headed, "Golf hustler's secret revealed." It goes on to make the confident assertion: "Here's what it *must* mean to you —30 yards on *every* drive." Another brand also claims to out-distance all other balls by 30 yards but adds, rather shamefacedly, that it is ever-so-slightly illegal. I'll have none of that malarkey but stick with my original choice at three for $5.

My guaranteed drive is now approaching a satisfactory 411 yards but there is more to come, for a ball-heater ("plugs into any standard electric outlet") promises me a 20 percent increase in distance, boosting me to 493 yards.

I am disappointed in the golfer's belt, which makes no promises about extra distance but merely offers the assurance of keeping my stomach ventilated during wear. However, the marvels of science have not yet exhausted their beneficence, and one of the major sources of extra length is to be found in the unlikely shape of the tee peg. At a paltry $2 for 18, the Slant Tee's bell-crank action propels the ball and promises me 10 percent more distance, giving me a guaranteed total of 542 yards.

But wait. The MighTee FlighTee not only will save me 75 cents but ensure me an extra 60 yards. And it is endorsed by Bob Toski, no less, giving me a grand total of 553 yards, every inch of it guaranteed by the advertisers. I must go with the MighTee FlighTee, especially as a later announcement adds, "Redesigned to conform with USGA regulations."

You may imagine that you have detected a flaw in my dream. Armed with the full cornucopia of mail-order goodies, I will drive too far, flying every green and sometimes by 200 yards or more. I have thought of that and shall adjust my equipment on every tee, sometimes using a cold ball or discarding my ankle shackle, so I reduce my potential to suit the length of the hole. But there is one gadget which I will use faithfully on every tee. If I have understood the illustration and description properly, it resembles a small handgun into which you load your tee peg. You then hold it against the surface of the ground and press a button which releases a pneumatic hammer to drive your peg into the earth. What a labor-saving device; the good ideas are always the simple ones.

"... and I'd like to thank my wife who kept
me from getting overconfident."

"Your five minutes are up, Fred."

"All I can tell you is he's supposed to be one helluva putter."

THE GREATEST FEAT IN GOLF HISTORY

by K. JASON SITEWELL

The beginning of April marks the 75th anniversary of what is probably the most spectacular feat in the history of golf. The records are uncertain whether it was March 31, 1900, or the next day (the only living witness of the event claims it was the latter).

It happened at the Imperial Golf Club in Melbourne, Australia. The principal characters were A. F. Daye, the leading British professional of his time, and Langley Corrigan, the local golf champion and winner of the Australian Open in 1899.

Both men were touring Australia in a head-to-head series. The match at Melbourne brought out a record crowd. Three matches had been played prior to Melbourne, Corrigan winning two of them. The people of the area were ablaze with excitement over the prospect that the local favorite would triumph over the vaunted Britisher.

The Melbourne course was a good test. Par 73. Length 7,900 yards. The toughest hole was the par-3 No. 17, reminiscent of the famous over-the-water 16th at Cypress Point in California, where many pros accept bogeys with equanimity, if not a spirit of thanksgiving. When players approach the 17th at Melbourne, they are close to a precipice; the drop to the floor of the canyon is about 1,200 feet. The green is 215 yards away. Usually, a strong wind whips in from the sea. Some of the longest hitters in golf have challenged the hole with a driver and fallen far short.

On this particular day, Al Daye was 1 up coming to the 17th. Corrigan was the first to hit. (In those days, the player who was behind in the match always hit first.) Playing it safe, Corrigan hit a 3-iron into the wind to the dogleg fairway on the short side of the gap about 170 yards away. He seemed certain to get no better than a bogey.

Daye saw a chance to wrap up the match right then. He was a long-ball hitter, outdriving Corrigan by 20 yards or more on most of the tee shots. He took out his 3-wood and challenged the canyon. The ball started out like a cannon shot; it appeared certain it would carry the green. When the ball reached its peak about 170 yards out, however, it hit gale-like reverse winds and fell about 10 yards short, plopping down to the canyon floor. Knowing he had lost the hole anyway and being stubborn, Daye took out his driver and belted a prodigious second shot that on an ordinary day would have carried at least 280 yards. The winds were now full force in the face of the players and the ball fell short again—this time by only six or seven feet. Daye decided on a third try—teed up, fired and missed.

Now the gale hit in full fury. Daye's caddie, an Australian aborigine of 61 years who couldn't have weighed more than 105 pounds, did something most unusual. He asked for permission to hit a ball over the ravine. Daye promptly put down a ball and offered his No. 1 wood, which the caddie spurned. All this time he had been carrying what appeared to be a walking stick. He turned it around and took a swipe at the ball which he had teed up very low. The swing was entirely original. The aborigine stood about 10 feet to the rear of the ball and then appeared to run at it, lashing at it with terrific velocity. It was a low, wind-cheating shot and easily made the green despite the long yardage.

Everyone was thunderstruck. When Daye recovered, he teed up a ball and invited the old man to hit again. Once again, the caddie ran at the ball like a javelin thrower, flinging himself at it, then springing into the air at the second of impact. This time, the ball was lost in the deepening fog and rain. No one knew whether it made the green.

The entire party started out for the other side, walking around the semi-horseshoe of the landscape to the green. When they got to the green, no ball was to be seen. The area around the green was flat and open; no ball there, either.

Then, suddenly, Corrigan began shouting incoherently. He was holding the pin and jumping up and down. Daye rushed up to Corrigan and demanded to know what the shouting was about. Still yelling, Corrigan jabbed at the hole with the pin. Daye looked down. Two balls were in the cup. Daye bent down for the balls, then looked up and smiled to the crowd. These were the two balls he had given the old man. Two successive holes-in-one by the same player on the same hole! Nothing like it had ever happened before (or has happened since). What made it all the more incredible was that it was done with a stick hardly the size of a walking cane. It later developed that the aborigine, whose name was Vrootengrud, had never played with regular clubs. He had used his cane for everything except putting.

As the result of Vrootengrud's double hole-in-one, hundreds of golfers would pilgrimage early in April each year to the site of the 17th tee. They would congregate close to the precipice and hold a sort of Quaker meeting, one of their number painstakingly recounting the episode. Inevitably, over the years, the story was embellished. One version described Vrootengrud as being 10 or 15

16

years older than listed. In another version, his son was the caddie and the old man was trailing along with the crowd, hobbling along on a cane, then stepping forward after Daye gave up, turning his cane around and bashing two balls across the long ravine into the teeth of the gale. According to this version Vrootengrud announced his feat in advance, much in the manner of Babe Ruth pointing to the bleachers just before swatting a home run against Chicago in 1932.

But these versions are plainly apocryphal. The true story is good enough just as it is and requires no embroidery.

The annual pilgrimages ceased with World War I in 1914. By that time the memory of the Vrootengrud feat had begun to recede. But a marble stone was erected at the site of the 17th tee memorializing the event. And the Australian Sportsman, which comes out the first of each month, publishes a short annual reminder of the event in its April issue. Last year, for example, the magazine ran a box in its editorial page which I reproduce herewith:

Vrootengrud Recalled

Seventy-four years ago on this date, the most spectacular feat in the history of golf, two successive holes-in-one, was performed by a caddie, Vrootengrud, believed to be 61 years old at the time. We honor his memory for the glory he has eternally brought to Melbourne.

The Vrootengrud legend is only slightly tarnished by something that came to light in 1905. Everyone had assumed at first that Vrootengrud had performed his feat with an ordinary walking cane, hitting the ball with the handle. Actually, he had used an authentic golf club of the variety in use during the early years of golf in Scotland; that is, a straight branch with a crooked neck. Vrootengrud had fashioned the club when he began to caddie as a youth of 13 and played with it regularly. After he turned 50 he became slightly arthritic and used the club as a cane.

It is not precisely accurate, therefore, to say that he hit his successive holes-in-one with a walking stick. Just the same, the truth detracts very little from the achievement. Even if he had made his successive holes-in-one with a modern graphite club, it still would have to be regarded as probably the most amazing achievement in the history of any sport.

About Vrootengrud himself: his glory, in a sense, turned out to be his undoing. Many players wanted to be able to boast they had been caddied by an old man who had performed a golfing miracle. Despite his worsening arthritis, Vrootengrud tried to accommodate everyone who asked him—not charging anything extra, even though he could easily have cashed in on his fame. His infirmity increased with the years, but he persisted nevertheless.

As might be expected, every time the players for whom he was caddying came to the 17th hole, Vrootengrud was asked to reproduce his feat. The old man was smart enough to beg off. He kept at his job until four days before his death at the age of 77. The obituary in the "A.S." gave the date of death as August 9, 1916.

To the end, Vrootengrud's only goal in life was to be a good caddie. That he achieved his purpose there can be no doubt.

"He shouldn't try to play after watching the long-driving contest."

THE TIN MAN TAKES A LESSON

by JAY CRONLEY

I needed a lesson. It came to me like that, like a sharp pain, one day on the third try at a 110-yard par 3. I need a golf lesson. I can Roman-candle them off the practice tee, and I sparkle them when it counts, but a lesson is what I needed .

The first lesson is the most difficult, not to absorb, but to submit to. It is an end of the I-can-work-it-out-in-a-day-or-two routine.

I wanted the entire county cleared for my first lesson, for fear somebody would see me being led by the hand through the wonderful world of golf, and here I had only been playing since I was 12.

I went to the pro, hands in pockets, head down, like a kid who had just been bad. I said I think I might need a lesson. Maybe. Perhaps.

The pro said we would see. He recorded my swing on video-tape, then replayed it. It is like seeing yourself eat. It was a picture of Houdini trying to escape from the suffocating grip of the mighty golf club. If you were not paying attention, you would have missed my backswing.

My right elbow was trying to ward off an unseen assailant. At the point of impact, my hands were running a badly beaten second to the clubhead. No contest. The follow-through was compact, so compact, in fact, that I almost hit myself on the jaw with my hands. I could have been hurt.

"Why didn't you follow the ball with the camera?" I asked. "It went great."

He said we needed a lesson. Didn't we though. Or a crowbar. We need to tie all the potentially capable parts together in a bow knot, so if anybody takes home movies, you will not hide your eyes.

"*You're kidding yourself,*" I said to myself.

"Yes, I know. I need a lesson to play better."

"*You saw what you looked like.*"

"Bad, huh?"

"*Worst I've ever seen.*"

"Well, let's go take a lesson. I'm not scared. Only, don't tell anybody, ever."

We began with the grip. I wanted to get right into the G-forces, but Golf Digest's illustrated instructions are frequently basic, so I went along with the professional. Also, with Golf Digest torn apart and spread on the living room floor, I play my apartment in 11 under.

He told me to hold the club. He said relax, it was my friend.

I said to me, *"That's it, I'm leaving."*

"Stay put."

"I feel like a fool. Next, we'll take a break for a bowl of pablum."

"It's costing $15, get your money's worth."

I looked at my grip. The "V" of my right thumb-first finger pointed at my left kneecap. That is a strong grip, too strong, way too strong. True, I could crush a Coors can, but I thought that was good. He moved my hand to the left. Is anybody looking?

He said hit a few with that grip. That is one good thing about lessons. Usually, they don't charge for the range balls.

I hit a few. With one swing. The ball went due right into other range balls. He said it would feel strange for a while.

"Strange? I felt like a gravedigger. I cannot get the clubhead through. I am going home. I am going to take up tennis."

"You took up tennis last year and you hurt your back."

"Oh, yeah."

"Get your guts up."

I hit six more practice golf balls with this foreign grip, each shot working its way left until the last one was only 75 yards off line.

The instructor told me to look at my left arm. He looked puzzled. He said I was not keeping the elbow stiff enough. He said if I didn't believe him, we could go look at movies. I believed him. He walked around behind me and we learned to dance and keep our left elbows straight.

"He's hugging me. He's going to kiss me. We're engaged."

"Pay attention. He is a pro, like a doctor. He's teaching you."

"Whew."

I told him I shot 72 twice last year, couldn't we get into something complicated. He asked how many times I shot 92. Not once on the practice tee, partner, I'll tell you that.

He backed away and I did the Tin Man act. All the joints were welded together. I was about to grind upper teeth into eyeballs.

Wait, wait, wait. The grip was back strong. Can't I listen? Don't I want to get better? He was put out with my impatience, and I was put out with his superiority.

I said that if I stayed with this grip, I will look like Carl Hubbell, and you will be able to spin my wrist like a doorknob. He smiled. He was human. We went on to the backswing, which was not human.

The top of my backswing is alleged. Nobody has ever seen it. I was told to stop the backswing before beginning the frontswing. Make it two movements.

"Yes, I have that. What do I do during the pause, dance?"

"You idiot, he just means a short pause so you will have control of the club."

"Why didn't he say so?"

"He is assuming you have some sense."

"He should be out raking traps."

Backswing. Pause. Hello there, little birdie, I am pausing during a backswing. What are you doing?

Stop, stop. Look at your hands, they're white. The club is not an enemy. Don't choke it. Loose grip. Remember the elbow. Remember the pause. Try it again.

Nothing to it. Do all that, then come up with a formula for making fuel out of coffee grounds. He is going to nickel-and-dime me to death with basics.

He said the swing was pretty good.

"Hey, this guy is OK. One thing, he knows talent."

"Don't get overconfident."

Now we were going to try this new and improved swing with a golf ball. Just think, I have been playing for 17 years, and now I get to swing at a golf ball for the video replay machine.

The golf ball seems smaller than usual. Quiet on the set. Take one: Cronley hits it for all he's worth. Action.

I wiggled a bit, the ham surfacing. I hit it. The ball, as you would expect, went right. Not correct, right. At the completion of the swing, I felt as if my body had been twisted at the midsection.

Cut. It's a take. Put it in the can. The Disney boys will love this one.

The film, when replayed, was remarkable in that it was a reasonable imitation of a competent golfer. When replayed after the swing recorded at the first of the lesson, I felt like a spin around the beach in search of bullies.

"I told you so."

"But all the results aren't in."

"At least you looked human."

"But it still goes right."

"But at least you know where it's going."

Time was up. Later, we would explore the mystery of the hips, the shoulders, the feet, even the mind. I hoped there were no math questions.

I have had seven lessons. I shall take three more. My films are all the way up to PG. I am confident enough to take lessons in public. I no longer ache.

"Hassim, your golf course came today."

"He has a great reputation for working with hopeless hackers. You should call him."

FOSTER DUPREE FINDS A NEW SWING IN VEGAS

by WILLIAM PRICE FOX

Only a few people in Savannah were really upset about Foster Dupree's deathbed scene. Most of them said, "After all, that's Foster. What did you expect?" Father Kelly, who was there at the end, was confused but kindly. "I've never understood golfers. I guess I never will."

But Foster's only son, Foster Jr., was still in shock. "Not in my wildest dreams did I ever believe he would do this to me. Never!" Foster Dupree was an hour out of Savannah on the night flight to Las Vegas. The other passengers were trapped listening to his story. "I'm the laughing stock of the town. Hell, my father didn't want a son. He didn't want someone to take over the business." He was loud and getting louder. "He wanted a golfer. A golfer! Golf, that's all he ever had on his damn mind."

The stewardess touched his shoulder. "You'll have to hold it down a little. OK, hon?"

"Absolutely." He finished his drink and handed her the glass. "Hit me again."

His voice lowered a bit but he was still addressing the entire first-class cabin. "You want to know why he married my mother?"

A chain-smoking insomniac in the dark corner raised his hand. "I'll bite."

Foster spread his arms in crucifixion. "She had a 10-handicap and could hit from left to right. It was a marriage made in heaven."

The insomniac lit another cigarette. "What did the old man have?"

Foster grimaced. "An 8. Can you picture an 85-year-old codger out there playing to an 8?"

The man moved forward and handed Foster his card. "What course was he playing?"

"The Savannah Inn." Foster checked the card. Monty Rosenthal, professional, Sunset Driving Range, Las Vegas.

Monty nodded, "I've played there. Great course from the white tees, fantastic from the blues."

"Dad played from the blues." Foster studied the card and slid

23

in close. "Maybe you can help me out." He was whispering. "Maybe this is more than just a chance meeting." Monty lit a cigarette with the glowing butt of the last. "You never can tell."

Foster sipped his brandy and began at the beginning. He was talking about his childhood. He told Monty how the slats in his crib were old wooden clubshafts. How his teething ring was a big dimpled Spalding Kro-Flight and that on his second birthday when he could barely cross the room by holding onto the couch the old man had presented him with a handmade set of clubs, a kangaroo skin golf bag and lifetime memberships at Augusta National and Maidstone out on Long Island.

Monty lit a cigarette and shook out the match. "Maybe you just didn't like golf?"

"No, at first I really liked it. I also liked baseball and basketball and tennis. But the old man would have none of it. It was all golf and nothing else."

They were coming out of Dallas when Foster decided to tell him about the deathbed and the terrible will his father had left. "You'll never believe it." He still couldn't believe it himself. It was an act of pure and absolute evil. He paused and stared at the Desert Inn poster on the bulkhead. On the poster a young tan warrior was playing with his girlfriend in the pool, a tennis player was coiling for a backhand at the net and two couples were drinking cocktails on a veranda overlooking the lush trees. The golf course was in the distance. The poster made him even sadder. The warrior had his girlfriend, the tennis player his backhand and the couples had each other. He had nothing but Monty Rosenthal, and the terrible chore that lay before him.

Monty cleared his throat. "You were saying."

Foster shook himself. "Oh, I'm sorry. Well, Monty, he was lying there up on the pillows and Father Kelly was with him with his cross and his Bible and his incense." He smiled thinly. "At first I thought the old bandit was coming to terms with Jesus. But then I see that Henderson is clicking off a slide show for him. He had this screen at the foot of the bed and was showing him shots of St. Andrews and Gleneagles and Winged Foot. I'd never seen them before." Foster's voice broke. "They were his favorite holes."

Monty's hand was on his shoulder. "If it's too tough let's forget it."

"No, I've got to tell somebody."

He finished his brandy and in the same smooth motion signaled for another. "You get the picture? Here's Father Kelly talking about the hereafter and Henderson clicking the carousel of slides and me standing there crying like a baby and he's rambling on about his damn golf holes."

"I got it."

"Well, Monty, he reached over and took my hand and then he said it. He said, 'Buddy'—he always called me Buddy when we weren't arguing—'when I'm gone you're going to hate me.' "

Monty said, "Jesus."

"He said, 'I've never been much of a father to you. I guess I saw you didn't have the turn and the timing and the big extension, and, well, I guess I just gave up on you. Maybe I was hasty. Hell's fire, maybe I was wrong.' Now, Monty, all the time he's talking he's giving me about 30 percent of his attention. The rest is up there on the screen; the 18th at Harbour Town, the third at Palmetto Dunes, the fifth at the Desert Inn. Then he says, 'Buddy, these are my dream holes. You won't understand this right now but maybe after you hear the will you'll shape up.'

"Then Henderson clicked the carousel and up came his tombstone on a hill overlooking the 18th at Savannah Inn. It read, 'Foster Dupree, 1893-1979. Handicap 8. Last round 84. Net 76. Lowest game 68, Gleneagles, April 7, 1937.' The inscription was for my benefit: 'Eagles do not give birth to doves.'

"The next shot was my tombstone. He had my death date open but he had me down for a 10 handicap. I leaned in and said, 'Dad, it says 10. I've got a 24.' Then he looked up. 'Buddy, it's going to be a 10 or you're not being buried with the Duprees.' And then, Monty, he actually grinned. 'And if you don't get down to a 10 you're not going to be in a lot of things around Savannah. It's all in the will.' "

Monty lit another cigarette and listened closely as Foster went on. "Well, Henderson had the 12th hole at Doral on the screen and Dad was mumbling how he'd birdied it in '62. Then it was the 13th at Baltusrol. And then I realized what was going on. Henderson had seen it too and was nodding. Father Kelly saw it and began praying. Dad was replaying his final round over his favorite holes. He finished the 17th at The Cascades and was on the 18th at Augusta. Henderson had handed him his old wooden-shafted putter.

"His voice was about to go but we could still hear him. 'I'm putting for a bird from the same place Jack beat Miller and Weiskopf.' Monty, those were his last words."

Foster stopped and looked out the dark window. In a few moments he told Monty how the old man had plumb-bobbed the hillside lie and laced his Vardon grip around the handle. Then he waggled one final time, holed out, smiled and departed. Foster paused, finished his drink and was silent.

Monty Rosenthal lit another cigarette. "That's the way to go."

By the time they saw the neon of Vegas, Foster had told Monty how the will stated that he was to play the Desert Inn course until he could play to a 10 handicap. They were on the approach leg and the No Smoking sign came on. Monty put his cigarette out. "From a 24? What if you can't do it?"

Foster was watching the lights of The Strip. "I keep the house, that's all. The business, the money, everything goes to some church in Atlanta. The Transcendental Unity of Inner Perception."

Monty said, "I never heard of it."

The plane landed and Monty was lighting up again. "So, say you can't pull it down to 10. Then what happens to you?"

Foster smiled like a long zipper slowly being opened. "It's terrible. I'll have to go to work." He cupped his hand over Monty's shoulder. "Listen, you know your way around. Maybe you can help me out?"

The pilot announced, "Ladies and gentlemen, welcome to Las Vegas. Have a nice evening and if you're driving, drive carefully and, oh yeah, good luck on the tables."

Then Monty grinned and slapped Foster on the back. "Foster, you're in luck tonight. If Monty Rosenthal can't straighten you out, no one can."

The next morning Foster met Monty at the golf shop. They signed in, changed shoes, checked out a car and cruised off to the first tee. The Desert Inn course is lush and long with nine kinds of roses, flowering trees and red, white and pink oleanders everywhere. With the tall palms swaying in the breezes and three new Titleists shining in the ball clip and two cans of cold Michelob in the drink holders, Foster's spirits were up and staying up. Maybe he could really do it? Maybe this strange, dark Monty was the miracle he needed. He felt younger, leaner, smoother, stronger. He sighed and stretched out luxuriously. "Monty, you drive. I want to enjoy this. Look at those mountains. This is God's country, it's really gorgeous."

Monty lit a cigarette. "It's the best."

As Monty addressed his ball, Foster smoothed on a new, white glove and watched the flag flapping on the green 495 yards away. It was a straight hole, no water and no trouble. As he tightened the glove strap he knew it was going to be a great day—a day he could play the game with anyone. Monty hit down the middle 220 yards. "Nice, Monty, nice. Now let me at it."

Foster lined up down the middle and squared his stance. His address and waggle looked professional and his takeaway was big and smooth. But suddenly Monty was ducking a screaming shank that headed like a streak for the parking lot. Monty's face was white. It stayed white as Foster did it again. On the third shot he skipped it down the right rough and they moved out.

Foster finally reached the green in eight and two-putted for a 10. Then it was three straight 7's and four straight 6's. On the ninth he holed out a 30-footer for a 5 and a front nine of 60.

As they left the ninth green Foster said, "Pretty bad, wasn't it? What do you think, Monty?" Monty looked up at the clouds. "I'll have to see a few more shots."

They headed for the 10th and Foster saw Sammy Davis Jr.'s golf car. "Hey, I've got to see this." He got out and circled it slowly. It was black with silver trim and a red shag rug interior. It was equipped with a tape deck, a TV set and a wet bar. The only thing missing was a beaded curtain and a water bed. Foster climbed back in the car. "Pretty funny, isn't it?"

Monty had something else on his mind. "Hilarious."

All during the round Foster kept asking Monty what he thought. And all during the round Monty kept answering, "Let me see a few more shots."

In the clubhouse under the photographs of Bing Crosby and Bob Hope in action, Monty spread out the scorecard. He looked at it calmly and lit a cigarette. Foster waited anxiously, knowing that this was it.

"Well, Monty, let's have it." He had had a 52 on the back side for a 112.

"Foster, you're a nice guy, but I've got a reputation around here. I'm sorry but I just can't handle you."

He paused and examined his cigarette closely, choosing his words carefully. "You've got just too many problems to deal with. There's no pattern I can work with. I'm sorry, Foster, there's just nothing I can do for you."

"Monty, if it's a question of money I'll be glad to pay you anything."

"No, that ain't the ticket. There's just nothing anybody can do with you."

"Well, then how about a referral. How about Greg Johnson, the pro?"

"I've already asked. He said it was impossible."

"But there must be someone out here who needs the money and knows something. Anyone, Monty, I can't do this alone. Man, I'm desperate."

"OK, I'll get you someone but I swear, Foster, I don't think it's going to work."

"Anyone, Monty, I'll take anyone."

Foster took four playing lessons from Monty's friend Sol for $1,000. From Sol's friend Marty he took four more for another $1,000. A week, then two weeks went by. There were other pros, other fees, other deals. He bought new clubs, new clothes, new shoes. He tried golf improvement encounter sessions, visited an astrologer on The Strip and even called an 800 toll-free number called Golf Crisis U.S.A., whose taped message was a pitch to sell him low-profile clubs and remind him to keep his head down. After 24 rounds Foster's score was still in the high 90's. He decided it wasn't worth it. He gave up.

He was at the Desert Inn bar for his last drink. As he pushed the ice around with the plastic stick he thought about how terrible it was going to be to ask his friends for a job recommendation. Who would he go to first? What would they think? What would they say? The piano player was doing a medley of Cole Porter songs and in the background he could hear the click-click of the roulette wheel and the thunking sound of the dollar slots.

At first he had liked the sound and the action and the neon but now he hated it and wished he'd never seen the place. It was stupid trusting a driving-range pro. It was stupid trusting any pro. But he'd not only brought it on himself, he had begged for it. He had been fresh meat and he'd walked into the butcher shop and said, "Take me." And they had. Foster sighed and rattled the ice in his glass. It was almost over now. He would have one last drink, check out and head back East. He would get a new lawyer and try to break the will.

And then someone said, "Foster!"

He turned around. "Monty!"

Monty sat down, shaking his hand. "You got a little sun, didn't you? Looks great."

"Yeah, but that's all I've got. I'm bailing out, Monty. I can't take it."

Monty looked over his shoulder. His voice dropped.

"That's why I came to see you. I think I've got someone who can do you some good."

"Not another pro, Monty. I can't afford him."

"No, nothing like that. Something bigger, something that will work. Now listen."

Foster listened and did exactly as Monty told him. He called from a pay phone out on The Strip and met a man in a red leisure suit in the parking lot. Silently he followed him to a private downtown club with no name. There the man pointed to a hallway and held up three fingers. He said one word, "Doors." Then he vanished. Foster opened the third door and as two men steadied two leashed Dobermans, he saw a very old and very fat man sitting behind an enormous desk. The man waved him in and Foster crossed the thick rug, slowly, not daring to look around.

The man handed him an ID card and a printed schedule. "Mr. Dupree, you will follow these directions to the letter. You will also call this number after your round for further instructions." He paused and closed his eyes. "Mr. Dupree, you will not talk of this to a living soul."

Foster felt a cold chill run up his spine as the words "living soul" hung in the air for three beats, four beats, five. He glanced at the 5:45 a.m. tee time on the directions. "I don't understand."

The man had a scholarly air about him. "Mr. Dupree, contrary to what the Germans say, understanding often produces even more confusion. Frankly, you're too far gone for understanding. Just do as you're told."

A Doberman growled and Foster said, "Yes, sir."

At 8 o'clock that night Foster saw the Tony Bennett dinner show at the Desert Inn. His ID card sat him in the best center seat in the house, and when Bennett sang "Georgia on My Mind," he sang it straight to Foster. After Bennett it was Sinatra himself at the Dunes, Kenny Rogers at the Riviera and Lola Falana at the Aladdin. The last show ended at 2. From there, following the directions, it was blackjack at the MGM, then poker at Caesars Palace, then craps back at the Desert Inn.

At 5:15, right on schedule and with no sleep, Foster had changed clothes and was on the first tee with Monty, waiting for the sun to rise and light the first fairway. On the first nine he had a 46. On the second a 45 for a 91. But now he was so tired he could barely climb out of the car to make the phone call.

The instructions were short and to the point. He and Monty were to check in the car and play the next 18 walking. They would carry their own bags. Foster couldn't believe what was happening to him. The first hole was agony, the second worse. He was too tired to walk, too tired to swing. Every time he squatted to tee the ball he thought he was going to pass out.

On the third hole he thought of telling Monty he was quitting. On the fourth he thought of not telling Monty and slipping through the oleander at the fifth tee and catching a cab to the airport. The hotel could have his luggage, his clubs and his bag. But then he remembered the Dobermans and the calculating look in the old man's eyes. He remembered the center seats, how even Sinatra had sung his southern song right at him and the way "you are not to tell a living soul" had hung in the air and scared him. He kept swinging and plodding on. He had forgotten why he was out there. All he wanted to do was finish, get in the hottest shower he could stand and get in bed and stay there. He was too weary to take a practice swing, too weary to swing hard.

It was a new swing, a dead man's swing based on deep fatigue and total indifference. He had left his umbrella and 2-wood at the starter's shack. At the halfway house he dropped off his 3-wood, his 2-iron, his sand wedge and one of his putters. He plodded on, swinging easy and trying to stay in the middle. And then on the 395-yard 12th he hit back-to-back long woods to the back of the green and was putting for a birdie. Foster didn't care if the ball went in or not—only that it didn't go too far and he'd have to recross the green. The ball hit the back of the cup and dropped. Monty said, "Great!" But Foster was looking around in a daze for the shortest way to the 13th.

When the round was over, Foster was too tired to put the dime in the pay phone. Monty had to do it for him. His hands and feet were swollen, his eyes were bloodshot, his face a raging red. As Monty dialed, Foster fell asleep against the booth. Monty shook him when the old man answered. He woke up begging, pleading. "Please, sir, I've got to get some sleep." "Nonsense, Mr. Dupree, you're doing splendidly."

The instructions were for another walking round. As Foster went back to the first tee he was seeing double and he was having hot flashes. The backs of his hands were itching. He knew he was going crazy. The swing based on fatigue and indifference was getting the ball out farther and straighter, but now Foster was too tired to see it.

After the fifth round it was 7:30. The neon was coming on and he could heard the disco music pounding from The Strip. He was propped up in the phone booth waiting for Monty to get the call through. Somewhere out on The Strip a big plane was revving up and somewhere close a mockingbird was trilling. The call went through. "Well, Mr. Dupree, what news do you have?"

Monty held the card so he could see it. An 82 was circled. Foster traced it left across the 5's, the 4's and the 3's. And there it was, his name, Foster. He looked at Monty. "Mine?"

Monty lighted a cigarette. "Right, yours."

Foster smiled into the receiver. "I think something's happening to me."

The man said, "Yes, I know. It's the legs. Now you're using them instead of riding on them."

Three days later Foster was still on the old man's schedule. He still hadn't slept. In the three days he had played 12 rounds and walked them all. He had played craps and blackjack and poker at every major club in town and had seen Sinatra again, Steve Lawrence and Eydie Gorme, Alan King, Shecky Green, Nipsey Russell, Liberace and Debby Boone. He was hollow-eyed and exhausted. He'd lost 10 pounds and was down to the usable muscle and nothing else. But he was happy. He was a new man. A new golfer. On the fourth day the old man let him sleep, but three hours in bed was all he could take; he had to be back out on the course.

It was five days later and Foster Dupree was on the 18th tee. He addressed the ball and started his big, new, easy swing. It was too dark to see the ball soaring against the clouds and bouncing out on the dark fairway, but he knew exactly where it would be— 220 down the left side away from the water on the right, exactly where he'd played it. He had played 26 rounds. The last 15 averaged 81.6 and Greg Johnson had given him an official USGA handicap of 9.

As he hitched up his bag and started forward, a low cloud was settling in over The Strip and reflecting the neon. It was a sight he'd seen once in the Mediterranean when they were sailing into Constantinople. But there the clouds were only pink and blue. Here they were the silvers, the golds and the reds and greens of the neon fireworks of The Strip and he could pick out the various clubs— the Stardust, the Sahara, the MGM, Caesars Palace and his favorite oasis in the West, the Desert Inn.

The ball was even with the 150-yard marker and he aimed a 6-iron at the lights behind the green. He hit and knew the shot was stiff. It would be a birdie for a 77 or a par for a 78. As he walked up in the dark, watching the reflecting neon and listening to the sounds of The Strip, he realized how wrong he'd been about his father. If he had only listened and tried harder and not frittered away the years with tennis and backgammon and polo. His father had been right; golf was the game, the only game. He'd also said that when golf was right, nothing mattered. When it was wrong, everything. Foster had the 9 handicap but now he knew he could get it down to an 8, a 7, maybe even a 6. He had the easy swing and the tempo and now he also knew he had the genes of the Savannah Duprees, whose big turns and high finishes went back to the time of Old Tom Morris and the glorious days of Bonnie Prince Charlie. The ball was six feet from the cup and he ran it in for a 3.

Inside the clubhouse Monty was at the bar. "How'd it go?"

"A 77 from the blues."

"Terrific." Monty lit a cigarette and blew a perfect smoke ring at the ceiling. "The old man wants to see you."

"Fine, I'd like to see him, too."

Foster met the man in the red leisure suit in the parking lot and silently followed him downtown. Once again he left him in front of the three doors and once again Foster eased by the Dobermans. The old man was sitting in a high-backed leather chair facing a deep leather couch. "Sit down, son."

Drinks were served and a tray of cheese was placed on the coffee table. Cigars were on the side. "I see you're close to a 7." Foster noticed his scorecards spread out on the big desk. "Yessir, and I want to thank you from the bottom of my heart. You have no idea how important this is to me."

"Yes, I do. You see, your father and I were the very best of friends. We were together in the war. Every year he would come out to see me."

"But he never mentioned you. I mean, I still don't even know your name."

The old man smiled. "I have many names. But that is of no consequence. Tell me, now, will you be coming back to see us? Las Vegas is very nice in December. The crowds thin out and the courses are beautiful. I can get you a very nice suite of rooms."

"You couldn't keep me away after what's happened to me out here."

"Lovely. Lovely. Now take this." The old man handed him an envelope. "You needn't open it here. It's the money you spent with the pros for the lessons. Monty Rosenthal is a very nice boy, but he makes friends with some boys who are, shall we say, not so nice."

For the next hour the old man talked about Foster's father. "He was a great man, Buddy. He told me to call you Buddy. His only regret was your game. Of course I kept after him to let me take care of it but he was just too good a father to force you. He was a wonderful man. A wonderful man." He poured out two more glasses of brandy. "My only wish is that we'd done this earlier." They sipped the brandy and the old man looked pensive.

"But maybe . . . maybe he knows it now. Yes, I somehow think he does. Buddy, one day you'll come to realize that golf is more than just a game. Right now, this very moment, I can feel his presence in the room." He smiled, "That's why I've laid out your scorecards."

He sat back and lit a cigar. "But maybe this is just an old man's pipe dream." He smiled again and rocked the brandy in the big glass. "But it gave me pleasure watching you swing out there. From a distance you're exactly like him. Buddy, it brought back many memories, many memories."

He reached out and took Foster's right hand. "Look, the thumb. If you'll move it a tiny bit more on the shaft you'll stop the movement at the top." He nodded with his eyes closed. "It was the same problem your father had."

Finally the old man said, "You must go now."

Foster stood up. "I'm going home for a few weeks and get things organized. I've decided to move out here."

"Splendid idea. Splendid. We'll get to spend a lot of time together. Yes, I'd like that very much. Very much. I'll tell you wonderful things about your father. Buddy, he was my closest and dearest friend. He always called me Don. Buddy, I want you to call me Don."

"I'll do that. And if there's anything, I mean anything I can do for you. I mean you've practically saved my life."

The old man's fingertips came together and his eyes twinkled. "Maybe one day you'll get a telephone call. Maybe not for a long, long time, but maybe soon. Then I'll ask you to do a favor for me." He closed his eyes and sipped his brandy. Then his eyes met Foster's. "Do you understand, Buddy?"

"Yes, and I'll be glad to do it."

"Fine. Your father would be proud of you. Goodbye, Buddy."

"Goodbye, Don."

The old man held up his right thumb. "Don't forget it. Just a tiny bit more on the shaft. It will make a world of difference."

"You sure surprised the gallery with that slice."

"That was my first hole-in-one."

WHO NEEDS MORE THAN THREE CLUBS?

by FRANK BOGGS

For as long as there have been printers, golf scorecards have stated that not more than one person may play out of the same bag. Fortunately, they do not say anything about one guy playing out of none. Not yet, anyway.

No bag is necessary when using only three clubs. Great for short evening rounds. . . .

"You must remember," said the kindly friend who has taken many strokes off my game, "that when you use only three clubs there will be some shots you will not have a club for." That seemed fair enough because always in the past there were 14 clubs I did not have shots for.

On my first effort, around a par-70 course, I shot 79, using the 8-iron, 3-wood and putter (it is important to take along the putter in case you do not hole out the 8-iron every time).

It was, of course, coincidence that I broke 80 for one of the rare times. The next day I decided to go all-out, having mastered the game. I took 14 clubs, three bag tags, one bag, one towel, an umbrella and two books of etiquette.

I rallied with a closing par, bogey, par. And shot 93.

Today, I am considered a disgrace. Professionals hate to see me arriving with three clubs when they are trying to sell 'em 14 at a time. Also, I no longer rent one of their golf cars because the strap in the back is too big to hold my three clubs.

I used to explain this deficiency to them. But I have quit trying to anymore because all the pros have told me so often where I CAN put my three clubs.

Actually, you might want to use only two clubs if you are a beginning golfer. I would suggest the 7-iron and a putter. Only when you master the game should you add the 3-wood.

In a short time these three clubs will become your best buddies. They are able to be out in the fresh air, same as you, rather than being hurled into the black bottom of a musty golf bag. They learn to pull off more different shots than their manufacturers knew existed.

Suppose, for example, you duck-hook the 8-iron too much. The

34

ball stops slightly short and to the left of the green. It is about 47 yards from the pin. You know this yardage figure because that morning, in the dew, you went out and stepped off precisely how many yards it was from the flagstick to where a well-executed duck hook would put you.

"Well," you say to your 8-iron, "ya feel up to a 47-yard shank?"

You take your stance, careful that you are lined up as if preparing to strike the ball to the next tee without completing the hole.

Then you simply hit a soft shank, the easiest of all golf shots to master. The shank is golf's most misunderstood shot. The secret is to take the proper stance before hitting it.

Another great benefit derived from the three-club theory is that you do not have to use up a lot of valuable concentration on club selection. The only decision to be made is whether to use the 3-wood or the 8-iron. Once on the green I find the putter is the choice, so there is nothing to think about there.

I suppose anyone using this system will wind up daydreaming. You soon chop another 10 to 12 strokes off your game, which means you are scoring somewhere in the mid to high 60's. You join the tour. You take the first-round lead somewhere and are invited into the press tent. Reporters want to know how you played each hole.

I can hardly wait.

"Well, on No. 1, I really busted myself a 3-wood, then I choked up about four inches and sliced a 3-wood into the rough, then closed the clubface on my 8-iron and hit a flyer 173 yards and dropped my putt for a bird . . . On the second hole. . . ."

"Bite!"

WHENCE COMES THE STRONG LEFT HAND?

by CHARLES BROME

There was no such thing as a golf glove anywhere in the world until one fine spring morning in 1066 when Henry VIII and the Iron Duke went out to the royal links for a friendly match.

A florin-florin-florin nassau, a shilling on birdies, sixpence on greenies (par-3 holes only) and a golden sovereign for the king just on general principles.

On the 11th tee the king sliced his drive way to hell and went out-of-bounds behind some trees which had been planted by the Crusaders to indicate the dividing line between England and Scotland. The Iron Duke was a comfortable six holes down at the time. He felt safe. He was generally acknowledged to be the greatest diplomat in the British Empire.

So he laughed.

"Stone the bloody crows," he chortled. "I've seen your majesty hit some rotten bloody shots in my time, but that one takes the bloody cake."

The king turned around slowly and looked at him.

The Iron Duke stopped laughing and started perspiring. He thought very, very hard for a moment.

Then he turned and glared at the king's caddie, who was really the royal headsman but who picked up some loose change now and then caddying when things were slow at the shop, which wasn't often.

"This poor bloody excuse for a caddie," the duke said indignantly, "must have slipped your majesty an American ball. That's got to be it. I don't think it's physically possible to make one of those dinky little British balls slice that much, no matter how bad a swing you put on it."

The king and the caddie-headsman just kept looking at him curiously. One of them (perhaps you can guess which one) smiled a little.

The Iron Duke coughed to clear his throat. Then he coughed to clear his throat again. Then he gave diplomacy one more try.

"Maybe," he said, "if Your Majesty would just have sense

enough to hit an iron off the tee the way I do . . . ." (That is why he was called the Iron Duke, of course. Any historian will tell you that. "Iron" because he always hit a pawky little iron off the tee, even on the par 5's, and "Duke" because he walked like John Wayne. Henry VIII got his name just by being the eighth son of remarkably unimaginative parents.)

The king nodded slightly to his caddie, who took a black silk hood and a nice, sharp, gleaming sand wedge out of the royal bag.

After a while the king went whistling off to look for his ball, a practically new Titleist.

He never did find it.

But in the course of his search he did happen across a bonnie Scottish lassie. She was milking a cow.

The king's keen eye noted that:

1. Eleven large oaken buckets were lined up nearby, each filled to the brim with fresh milk. The milkmaid was plugging grimly away on No. 12.

2. The cow seemed to be pretty much your standard cow, but it had a curiously drawn, shrunken look about it. On its face was an expression of pure desperation.

3. Upon close inspection, the lassie was not really all that bonnie. The only thing about her to draw a second royal look was the glove she was wearing on her left hand.

4. The glove was strangely and marvelously wrought of purple imitation-leather plastic. Inscribed across the back in large, flowing gold script was the mystic legend "Kenneth Waterman Model" and on the inside, stamped in very tiny letters and partially obscured by the patented snap fastener, the words "Made in Hong Kong."

"Prithee and odds bodkins," said the king, who could turn on the old charm when he wanted to, "would'st tell me how you managed to squeeze all that milk out of one lousy cow?"

Without pausing in her work, the milkmaid lifted the cow into the air with her left hand and pointed at the glove with her right.

"It improveth my grip," said she.

The cow, suspended resignedly in midair, provided mute testimony that she indeed spake the truth.

So the king took the glove away from her and went back to the 11th tee, where he was now shooting three.

He put on the glove and hit the greatest drive of his life, straight down the middle and with a slight draw at the end that gave him an extra 10 to 15 yards.

During the next fortnight his handicap went from a shaky 43 down to scratch.

He qualified for the British Open, made the cut nicely and was well on his way to winning the championship until he ran into a crazy American with an enchanted pitching wedge.

When he died, he died a happy man.

"Actually, I can't see any of us deserving the honor."

"Five thousand bucks?!!!"

THE INVENTION OF ARNOLD PALMER

by DAN JENKINS

The first time any of us ever actually noticed a guy named Arnold Palmer was on the veranda at Augusta around 1957 and we wondered who that vacationing longshoreman was talking to Bob Drum, the writer.

Later Drum said, "That's Arnold D. Palmer of Latrobe, Pa., the next great golfer."

"Yeah, sure," one of us said. "And I'm the next Steinbeck. But first I got to get me some of those maroon pants with the cuffs turned up, and a green shirt, and an orange alpaca, like your pal over there. Arnold who?"

There were only two golfers then, we liked to joke: Hogan and Snead. Well, maybe there was a Middlecoff occasionally. Writers are very strict about touring pros having familiar names. Editors make writers take laps and do push-ups when Jack Fleck or Orville Moody wins a U.S. Open.

In any case, I was convinced our next hero of the era would be Ken Venturi. Others fancied Gene Littler.

"Venturi perhaps," Drum would say. "But there's no such guy as Littler. He mails in his scores. Arnold D. Palmer of Latrobe, Pa., is the next great chin. He makes 4,567 birdies a day."

Usually, when Drum spoke, you were forced to listen. He was larger than all of the rest of us put together, he could outdrink the British army without showing it, and he was one of the more entertaining writers on the golf circuit. At least he was to those of us who were familiar with the Pittsburgh Press, or who would read over his shoulder as he sat typing in the pressrooms roaring with laughter at his own words.

I should point out right here, I think, that it is impossible to reminisce about Arnold Palmer without continually thinking of Bob Drum, of whom an army captain once said, when Drum was defending our country by teaching Nazi prisoners how to play softball in Italy and North Africa: "You're aptly named, Drum. Big, loud and empty."

That was wrong. Drum was big, loud and hilarious, and he

merely introduced most of us to half of the people in the world that we know. As I have said over many a cocktail through the years, "Bob Drum *invented* Arnold Palmer."

That statement will of course ring with accuracy only to anyone in the profession of journalism. No one really invented Arnold Palmer, naturally, except Mr. and Mrs. Palmer. But if ever an athlete had an unofficial publicity and public relations director who could do a job for him—purely out of friendship, admiration and no doubt a little hero worship—Arnold had such a man in Bob Drum. And Arnold had him in the days when it mattered the most—when Arnold was becoming the Arnold of "Whooo, haaaa, go get 'em, Arnie."

Writers have golfers, you know. And golfers have writers. In a way, I suppose, a lot of us thought of ourselves as a modern-day version of O. B. Keeler, who had Bobby Jones.

Ben Hogan belonged to everyone, to be sure, but I certainly felt he belonged mostly to me. I was from the Fort Worth Press, and Ben was the reason I started going to the big tournaments. My assignment in those days, therefore, was to follow Hogan, shot-by-shot, quote-by-quote, and, secondarily, to cover the tournament proper.

In so doing I became a sort of Hogan walking bibliography, which is what our old friend, the late Walter Stewart of the Memphis Commercial-Appeal, became with Cary Middlecoff. It is what Kaye Kessler has become in Columbus with Jack Nicklaus, and what Art Spander has become in San Francisco with Johnny Miller. And it is what Bob Drum was in Pittsburgh with Arnold Palmer.

Drum and I became friends back in 1951. We first met trying to avoid a drink check on the Masters veranda. Possibly, we became friends because I could supply him with Hogan quotes and he could give me Snead quotes. I didn't know Snead well. He was the enemy.

Drum would say to me, "Hey, Texas," as he typed on deadline. "Gimme a Hogan quote."

If I didn't have any yet, I would invent one. If Drum didn't like it, he would yell, "I read that in Herbert Warren Wind's book, you rotten son of a bitch. Gimme something fresh."

Ultimately, together, Drum and I would come dangerously close to making Ben Hogan out to be a stand-up comedian in the Pittsburgh Press and the Fort Worth Press.

I recite all this only to prepare the world for the confession that Drum and I, over the years, did as much for Arnold Palmer. As Drum was saying recently, "He thinks he *said* all those things."

An example of *all those things* would be this: The brilliant journalists are on deadline, Arnold has won the Masters again, and it's time for a human voice to appear in our copy, but we haven't spoken to Palmer yet.

Let's say this is 1960, as Drum and I are blazing away on the typewriters. Couldn't anyone tell by the smoke? Faster. The stories are eating away at the cocktail hour.

"What did he say?" I would ask.

"He said Augusta's a par 68," Drum would babble, typing it. "He said he's going to the British Open. He said the modern professional Grand Slam is the Masters, the U.S. Open, the PGA and the British Open."

"Arnold Palmer said that?" I asked.

"Who the hell are we talking about?" Drum said. "Laurie Auchterlonie?"

Thus, Arnold Palmer would read in the Pittsburgh Press that he would go to the British Open. He would also learn what the Grand Slam was. In a roundabout way, it was Bob Drum who rejuvenated the British Open, for when Arnold started going, everybody else who mattered did.

Much has been written about Palmer at Cherry Hills in 1960, of what he said in the locker room before going out for the final round of that U.S. Open when he shot the 65—and shot down the field. Arnold never actually made a serious prediction that day. He was too far back; practically out of the tournament.

Drum and I found Arnold sitting on a bench in the locker room. He was sitting there with Venturi and Bob Rosburg. They were eating hamburgers and drinking iced tea. We stumbled across them, in fact. We had been looking for Mike Souchak, the leader.

The three of them were joking around, as players do who are out of contention. We simply sat down to listen. Eventually, Arnold got around to talking about how much Cherry Hills' first hole "bugged him," as he put it.

"You ought to be able to drive that thing," Arnold said. "With the right bounce over the rough, you could get it on there."

It was a par four.

"Sure," Drum said. "If you're George Bayer in a limousine."

"I've almost been on it," Palmer said.

"I've almost been on it in two," said Venturi.

It went along like this for a few more minutes, or until it was time for Arnold to tee off for the last 18.

He stood up and smiled at Drum.

"You coming?" he said.

Drum said, "I'm tired of watching duck hooks. There's a guy named Souchak leading the tournament. He's from Pittsburgh, too."

"If I drive the first hole I might shoot 65," Arnold said.

"Good," said Drum. "You'll finish 14th."

"That would be 280," Arnold said. "Doesn't 280 always win the Open?"

I said, "Yeah. When Hogan shoots it."

Arnold laughed and left.

He had driven the first green and birdied the first four holes before Drum and I caught him and climbed, sweaty and out of breath, under the gallery ropes, as our armbands permitted.

As we loitered on the fifth tee, Arnold took the Coke in a paper cup out of my hand and sipped on it. He took a pack of cigarettes out of my shirt pocket and lit one.

He did say, at that point, and with a grin, "Fancy seeing you here."

But he didn't say, "Who's winning the Open?" He said that a few holes later, after he had birdied six of the first seven and had noticed that *he* was leading the Open.

As much as I would like to give Drum the credit, Bob did not originate "Arnie's Army." A young fellow named Johnny Hendrix did in the Augusta Chronicle. Drum immediately recognized the historical importance of it, however.

As we were reading the paper one morning during the Masters in the old Bon Air Hotel coffee shop, Drum said, mostly to himself, "I'll be a son of a bitch. Here's a mush mouth from the South like you who's just made himself immortal."

There was a pause, and Drum said:

"Arnie's Army, comma."

I was fortunate to get to know Arnold early, me being the guy who was always with Drum. When he captured his first Masters, in 1958, I got to be with Arnold and Winnie that evening, as Drum and I earnestly sought our "Monday follow-ups."

When he took the British Open at Troon in 1962, Arnold celebrated by having a reasonably quiet dinner with Winnie, Drum and I in the dining room of the Marine Hotel. I remember the staff sending over a cake to the table with an inscription in icing: "Open Champion." Arnold sliced the cake, took a piece, stood up, smiled at the room and sat down.

Whereupon he turned to us and asked:

"Do you suppose I have to eat it?"

I can still see him in the parking lot at Oakmont in 1962 after he had lost the U.S. Open playoff to Nicklaus. He's angry. He's slamming the clubs in the trunk of the car.

"You three-putted 12 greens in the tournament," I said. "He only three-putted once."

"Screw statistics," said Drum. "The fat kid can play golf."

The competitor came out in Arnold.

"I can beat the fat kid the best day he ever had," Arnold said.

On our way back to the press tent, I said, "That was a hell of a quote."

Drum laughed, agreeing.

"And we didn't make it up," he said.

We were in Arnold's home in 1966 not too long after he had blown the Open to Billy Casper. Nobody could blow seven shots in the last nine holes to anybody, but Arnold had.

"I could have played safe," Arnold said, "but that wouldn't have been me. That's not how I got where I am. He kept playing safe even when he was catching up. I couldn't believe it."

Drum said, "If you'd played safe and won, we'd have said you were a dirty, rotten coward."

Arnold roared laughing. It helped.

As late as 1959 I was still not convinced that this guy from Latrobe, who so far had only taken one Masters, was going to be The Man. And just as I was about to be convinced, on that Sunday in Augusta, as Arnold was leading going to the 12th tee, on the verge of winning the Masters two years in a row, catastrophe struck —and almost took Drum with it.

We were up on the press tower which overlooks the 11th green, and all of the par-3 No. 12. It is not an exaggeration that when Arnold hit his shot into Rae's Creek at the 12th hole—he would take a double bogey and blow the whole thing—Drum lost his balance in an emotional struggle to hurry the ball over the water.

I recall hearing, "Aaada . . . got . . . son of a . . . eeeiiiii . . . ," as all 260 pounds of Bob Drum fell off the tower.

In his glory days Arnold Palmer was probably the most gracious and friendly of any superstar ever. He was forever helpful and had time for any writer, whether the writer's name was Drum or not.

I never saw him refuse to sign an autograph for a fan, no matter how inconvenient it might be, no matter how obtuse the person.

One of the reasons was because Arnold was just naturally a good-natured individual. But another reason, after he became Arnold Palmer, was because Bob Drum frequently schooled him on how to handle himself. Or teased him into doing the proper thing. Or joked him into it. Or provoked him into it.

There was the year when we were all in Las Vegas at the Tournament of Champions, when Arnold wanted to go home. He wanted to skip Colonial, an event to which I was obviously partial, it being in my old home town of Fort Worth.

"You've got to play Colonial," said Drum. "It's in our friend's town." He meant mine.

"I'm worn out," Arnold said.

After a while, Drum said, "You don't want to go because you can't play the golf course. It's too tough. You can't play a tough, narrow course."

You could almost hear Arnold growling. He went on to Colonial, and, incidentally, won the tournament.

Not too many seasons ago, during the Los Angeles Open, I was expected to do a rather lengthy television interview with Arnold for a show which was co-sponsored by the magazine I work for, Sports Illustrated. I explained to Arnold that he would be doing it for free, and that it would probably require an hour. It was being set up for the next day, after he completed his round.

"I'll have to clear it with Mark," he said, meaning Mark McCormack, through whom he had been clearing his empire for years.

It was a doubly uninviting thing for Arnold to do because we would be talking about why he wasn't winning anymore.

The following day when I approached him, he said, "I talked to Mark and I'm afraid I can't do it. There's a complication with another network and some other reasons you're aware of."

I said, "Forgetting business, why don't we just look at it as a personal favor to me?"

Arnold fidgeted with that thought for a while as we had a drink, and finally he said:

"Aw, hell. Let's do it anyway and not tell Mark."

In the great years when he seemed to win whenever he was in the mood, or whenever it was important, he earned a sort of underground nickname among a few of us. Bubba.

I think it must have been around 1962, and, again, at Augusta, when it happened. More things have happened to Palmer at Augusta than have happened to Bob Drum on side streets.

Anyhow, neither Drum nor I will soon forget Arnold lining up a birdie putt on the fourth green at Augusta during the playoff with Gary Player and Dow Finsterwald. Near us behind the ropes, among the hordes, was your basic southern golf fan, all decked out in cap, cleats, hotdog, binoculars, sunburn and accent.

Quietly, the fan said:

"You make this one, Bubba, and you da leader of da tribe."

Bob Drum and his trusty sidekick, me, and a few others in our drinking and typing club, have been calling him "Bubba" ever since.

But Arnold Palmer, whose wife calls him Arn, and whose army calls him Arnie, has never known why.

Now that all of us mostly deal in memories, since Drum no longer writes for a paper and Arnold seems unable to win the big ones, we will have to tell him that one of these days.

"You were the best, Bubba," Bob Drum will conclude, raising a glass of vodka. "There was no such sport before you came along."

And I will agree, smiling at them both with immense pleasure and fondness.

"Hey, Mike. You forget we had a game today?"

"It's a long story."

THERE'S NOTHING LIKE A ROUND WITH THE KIDS

by LARRY SHEEHAN

With so much talk about junior golf these days, I thought I would investigate firsthand. I took my son Alex and his pal Joe, both 11, out for their very first nine holes of golf—or field hockey in the case of how they played most of the longer holes.

Anyway, here in no special order are the things I learned about the phenomenon:

Kids think a divot is a club.

Kids think putting is a bore.

If they must putt, kids prefer leaving the flagstick in.

Kids don't take long to begin to sound like golfers. "I'm not getting them up in the air today," said Joe on the second hole. "I think I'm spinning out."

Kids like to push pullcarts, not pull them.

Kids don't care for walking up steep hills.

Kids fear sand traps above all else.

Kids also worry a lot about hooking the ball. "Oh no, I hooked it," said Joe after topping a 3-wood. "Look at that, it hooked," said Alex, upon leaving a putt short.

Kids take a lot of practice swings.

Kids call whiffed shots "practice swings" just like everybody else.

Kids are brutally unsentimental about their equipment. Once, after Alex slightly mis-hit two consecutive shots with his 7-iron, he simply gave the club to Joe, explaining, "It doesn't work for me anymore."

Kids are never ready to hit. Instead, they're eating Oreo cookies, killing frogs in lateral water hazards, tying the laces on their Pumas or washing golf balls.

Kids think ball-washing devices are the greatest invention since sliced bread. And they use them at every opportunity, usually during your backswing.

Drinking fountains come in a close second to ball washers as things to flock to on the golf course, even if they're two fairways across from where you're playing.

Kids like to get down on their hands and knees to tee up the ball.

Kids tee off in the order in which they can locate their drivers, which often are left somewhere along the previous hole.

After teeing off, kids always forget to put the wooden tees back in their pockets and have to run back to the teeing area to collect the items which are rightfully theirs and should not be left for someone else.

For reasons such as the above, kids are slow and must let other golfers play through on every other hole. But that's all right, this gives them more time to look for frogs.

Kids are tolerant of each other's misfortunes on the course. Alex broke into gales of laughter only one time—when Joe stepped into casual water up to his knees. Joe fell down in hysterics just once, too, after Alex managed to hit the same tree twice on successive shots.

But maybe this was because I had held their naturally competitive natures in check by prohibiting scorekeeping from the start. I hadn't wanted them getting on each other as I had seen them do numerous times on the tennis court, for example. Nor did I want them to feel they had to compete with me and my 25 years of experience in the game.

We kept score only on the last hole when I knew it would be too late to do any real harm. So I made 6, my son tied me and his friend trailed by one.

"Don't worry, Joe," said Alex as we walked off the green. "You'll get him next time."

"Yes, I know what tomorrow is. It's Arnold Palmer's birthday."

THE YIPS—
ONCE YOU'VE HAD 'EM,
YOU'VE GOT 'EM

by HENRY LONGHURST

There can be no more ludicrous sight than that of a grown man, a captain of industry perhaps and a pillar of his local community, convulsively jerking a piece of ironmongery to and fro in his efforts to hole a three-foot putt. Sometimes it is even a great golfer in the twilight of his career, in which case the sight is worthy not of ridicule but of compassion. He will battle on for a year or two, but twilight it is, for "once you've had 'em, you've got 'em." I refer, of course, to what Tommy Armour was the first to christen the "yips."

When he wrote a book called "The ABC's of Golf," he had no difficulty with the letter Y. The yips drove Armour out of tournament golf. On a somewhat humbler level they drove me out of golf, too, and a long and agonizing process it was, ending on D-Day, 1968, the anniversary of the invasion of Europe. On that occasion I put my 25-year-old clubs up into the loft with the water tanks, where they remain.

Armour wrote graphically of "that ghastly time when, with the first movement of the putter, the golfer blacks out, loses sight of the ball and hasn't the remotest idea of what to do with the putter or, occasionally, that he is holding a putter at all." This confirms the description of that most distinguished of all sufferers, Bob Jones, who recorded that just before the moment of impact the ball "seemed to disappear from sight." Jones also recorded how he once was partnered with that sterling character of the late 1920's and early 30's, Wild Bill Mehlhorn. Poor Mehlhorn! He was only three feet from the hole, said Jones, but gave such a convulsive twitch at the ball that it shot across the green into a bunker. He then had the humiliation of exchanging his putter for his niblick, and, we may assume without being unkind, that was the last seriously competitive round he ever played.

Contemporary with Jones and Mehlhorn was Leo Diegel, whose extraordinary spread-elbowed putting style put a new phrase into the golfing vocabulary—"to diegel." I watched him on

48

the 18th green at St. Andrews in 1933 when, from some yards above the hole, he had two to tie for the British Open title. While his partner holed out, Diegel paced up and down, much as an animal in its cage, repeatedly taking off his felt hat and mopping his brow. When his turn came, he charged the ball down the slope, several feet too far, chased after it and, almost before it had come to rest, yipped it a foot wide of the hole. Everyone knew, as I am sure he did, too, that Diegel would never win an Open now.

Armour wrote, "Yips don't seize the victim during a practice round. It is a tournament disease." Here the great man was certainly wrong. My mind goes back to a conversation at Augusta with Craig Wood, who was robbed of the 1935 Masters by Gene Sarazen's historic double-eagle. Craig told me that he even got the yips on the practice green, all by himself and with nothing at stake. Again, Armour says, "I have a hunch that the yips is a result of years of competitive strain, a sort of punch-nuttiness with the putter." Wrong again, surely, for you will see any number of compulsive yippers, though many may not admit it, in Sunday foursomes whose members never play serious competitive golf at all.

In winning the 1931 British Open Armour, having perpetrated a most frightful yip to miss from two feet on the 71st hole, found himself faced with a three-footer to win. "I took a new grip, holding the club as tightly as I could and with stiff wrists, and took a different stance . . . From the instant the club left the ball on the backswing I was blind and unconscious." Next day that greatest of golf writers, Bernard Darwin, recorded in The London Times that he had never before seen a man so nonchalantly hole a three-foot putt to gain a championship!

Who, would you guess, wrote the following, and in what book?

"As I stood addressing the ball I would watch for my right hand to jump. At the end of two seconds I would not be looking at the ball at all. My gaze would have become riveted on my right hand. I simply could not resist the desire to see what it was going to do. Directly, as I felt that it was about to jump, I would snatch at the ball in a desperate effort to play the shot before the involuntary movement could take effect. Up would go my head and body with a start and off would go the ball, anywhere but on the proper line."

That was written by Harry Vardon, winner of six British Opens and one U.S. Open, indisputably the greatest golfer that the world had yet seen. And the book was entitled "How to Play Golf"!

Americans sometimes refer to the yips rather unkindly as "whisky fingers," and sometimes no doubt they are. Perhaps the last word on "whisky fingers"—and almost my favorite golfing quotation—was uttered by Vardon to a lady who was trying to persuade him to sign the pledge. "Moderation is essential in all things, madam," said Vardon gravely, "but never in my life have I been beaten by a teetotaler."

Sam Snead, whose fluent style has lasted longer than any other man's in the history of the game, was reduced to putting between his legs, croquet-fashion—and he was a total abstainer for years. The croquet putter gave many a golfer, myself included, an extended lease on life and the banning of it was an act of cruelty to many hundreds of miserable wretches for whom the very sight of a normal putter set their fingers twitching. The ease with which you could line up one of these croquet putters to the hole was quite remarkable. By holding the club at the top with the left hand, thumb on top of the shaft, and loosely lower down with the right arm stiffly extended, the most inveterate yipper could make some sort of stroke at a four-foot putt which would not expose him to public ridicule. We did not ask to hole it; all we wanted was to to be able to make a stroke at it, and this we could do. The United States Golf Association not only decided to ban a method which had brought peace to so many tortured souls, but the group let its decision become public before the Royal and Ancient Golf Club of St. Andrews had time to consider it, thus putting the latter in the impossible position of either banning the club or falling out with the USGA. So they banned the club.

Further proof that the dread disease is not traceable to a dissolute way of life was furnished by the "Iron Man" of golf himself, Ben Hogan, who of all the men who have played golf since the game began would have seemed most likely to be immune. The rot set in, so eye-witnesses have assured me, on the 71st green at Rochester in 1956, when he was well-placed to win a record fifth U.S. Open. Not only did he miss the three-footer, which anyone could do, but he yipped it, and that was the beginning of the end. At any rate, my last memory of Hogan in competitive golf was at the Masters some years ago. Every green, as usual, is surrounded with spectators and, as the familiar white-capped figure steps through the ropes, everyone spontaneously rises to give him a standing ovation. And a moment later he is struck motionless over the ball, as though hypnotized, unable to move the ironmongery to and fro.

Is there any cure for this grotesque ailment? Few people can have made a more penetrating research than myself. The first led me to a psychiatrist-cum-hypnotist, who solemnly tried through my inner self to talk the ball into the hole. This, of course, was ridiculous since all I was seeking was that, on surveying a four-foot putt, a massive calm should automatically come over me instead of the impression that I was about to try to hit the ball with a live eel.

Better hope came from an Austrian doctor, who wrote to say that he knew the solution and would be willing to reveal it to me. Within a matter of hours I was visiting him in his rooms in London. "It all comms," he said, "from ze angle of ze right ell-bow." Something in that, I thought, recalling how, with the right arm stiffly extended, one could at least make some sort of stroke with the croquet putter. The theory seemed to be supported by the fact that, if you have difficulty in raising a glass to the lips, it is when the arm bends to approximately the putting angle that your drink is most likely to make its bid for freedom.

What he said next, however, blissfully unaware of the full horror of his words, was "Violinists very often get it." We may imagine a silent audience of 6,000 people in, say, London's Albert Hall and the maestro in the spotlight, his right arm fully extended, drawing the bow delicately across, when suddenly, the elbow having arrived at the putting angle . . . A-a-a-ah! He nearly saws the instrument in half and his career is ended. I once told this ghastly little story to Ben Hogan during a World Cup match and thought his eyes began to turn glassy. Only later did I suspect why.

Innumerable "cures" for the yips have been tried and passed on from one sufferer to another: Looking at the hole instead of the ball; putting left-handed; putting cross-handed with the left hand below the right, and putting with the hands wide apart (probably the best bet of the lot). A friend of mine has his hands about a foot apart, with the left below the right, and then pulls down as hard as he can with the left and up as hard as he can with the right—and he a one-time runner-up in the British Amateur.

But the bitter, inescapable truth remains. Once you've had 'em, you've got 'em.

"Then it's agreed, gentlemen. A dollar nassau with automatic presses when 2 down, and no mulligans or in-the-leather gimmies on Saturday."

"In the rule book it's just listed as a falling coconut hazard."

AMERICA'S CRUMMIEST COURSES

by DAN GLEASON

Some golf courses leave the feeling that they weren't so much designed as simply part of some disaster a long time ago. When the touring pros talk with such awe about Butler National, it makes some of us wonder whether they actually understand what tough is. When Arnie talks about playing with courage, I wonder whether anybody has ever tried to shove him into a ravine or pull the watch off his wrist when he is lining up an important putt.

As a matter of fact, there are plenty of courses that, in their own special ways, are much more challenging than anything the pros ever play. Here are my own worst courses. This account is based on real places, but I would have to admit, if closely pressed, that my imagination may have intruded a bit now and then.

Batting helmet a must at this Brooklyn course
Space becoming such a problem these days, especially in the industrial northeast, a public course in New York has set a stunning example of conservation. Eighteen holes have been squeezed into an area formerly occupied by nine.

Undaunted, Bermuda-shorted, black-socked veterans have taken to wearing hard hats along the crowded fairways. The pro shop does a brisk business selling Mets batting helmets for $3.75, and caddies have taken to carrying shield-like devices.

It isn't easy to win an award for having "America's Fastest Hole," but this Brooklyn course is a cinch. The owner put up lights on the first three holes, enabling the first tee time to be moved back from 5:30 a.m. to 4:22 a.m. A turnstyle was installed and an assistant pro stationed on the first tee with a starter's pistol. The first 75 yards of the hole were paved, and groups allowed just 90 seconds between tee-offs.

The course has averaged 46 more groups per day.

Looking for a thrill? Try Hola-Amigo in Texas
If you're looking for a wild time, the 14 members of Hola-Amigo Golf and Country Club in west Texas can show it to you. Lack of

funds has not stopped these lighthearted, fun-loving pipeline workers from operating their golf club the way they see fit.

The club has had temporary tees since 1964, and the neighboring Flying-A truckstop serves as an adequate clubhouse. In 1972, four-time club president Pudge Outlar ran the club treasury up in a poker game, bought two little Crosley cars from a junkyard, cut the tops off them and made them into golf cars.

The waitress who runs the golf shop says that people come from all over to watch the club championship. "It's the big day around here," she said. "We do a big business. All the oil riggers show up to have a good time. We hold the preliminaries in the morning and the finals in the afternoon. It's hot, and everybody drinks plenty, and by noon they're fightin' to see who gets to fight *you*. But it's all clean fun and they pay their damages.

"One time I remember a fella was down at the Trailways depot waitin' on a bus and they just said, 'Come on and play in the club championship.' That's the kind of guys we got out here. That fella might've won, too, if he hadn't got shook on the last two holes."

The members load up the two Crosleys with beer and drink straight shots of tequila with beer chasers. They play in their cowboy boots and work shoes and take along rifles to shoot at prairie dogs and rattlesnakes. By the time they hit the last two holes, they're usually prepared for anything—and they get it.

The eighth hole was built on a mesa, and the chopped-down Crosleys aren't powerful enough to climb it, so the players must make their way up on foot.

But it's the ninth that's the tester. It's 530 yards long and almost straight down off the mesa. There are no sand traps because the wind would blow the sand away, but there are plenty of mesquite and prickly pear traps. The members have cut off old car hoods and fashioned sleds for the ride straight down through the cactus at speeds of over 60 miles an hour.

The members play a game called "Survival" wherein the man with the highest score on the 18th hole has to stand out 180 yards in the fairway while the rest of the group gets to hit three balls apiece at him. He's allowed to duck and twist and cover his head, but he can't move his feet.

"You know," one of the members remarked, "I don't think people back east know how to have a good time."

Jersey boasts America's most dangerous course

There is a rather distinguished course hard by the Jersey swamplands that not only boasts two of America's crummiest holes, but by realistic standards *the* toughest hole in the western world. And almost as astonishing is the fact that the course does not have a name, as such, just a neon sign that flashes off and on, off and on: PIZZA-GOLF.

The neighborhood has such a high crime rate that the clubhouse windows are protected with iron bars. The man who runs the shop takes your money from inside a little cage behind the counter. If you buy golf balls, he holds the balls out through an opening in the cage. The instant you grab the balls, he grabs the money, then slams the sliding window shut. If you fake with your money, he fakes with the balls.

It's also treacherous out on the course, and it's the seventh hole that earns the title of tough. It's only 287 yards, the fairway is flat and there are no traps. But it's the farthest hole away from the clubhouse, and the out-of-bounds is alongside a rundown housing project. Neighborhood gang members frequently climb the high fence that protects the hole on the right.

The aware golfer could save himself a hard time by wearing a cheap watch or some imitation jewelry. A pocket knife, perhaps some spare change or a bottle of Spanada wine in the shag bag isn't altogether a bad idea. It's an excellent opportunity to get rid of those comp golf balls the oil companies hand out.

Par is four, but the hole plays two strokes tougher near dark.

Although the finishing ninth hole isn't as dangerous physically, it's no less a challenge. The course was built over what was once a city dump. Old tires and garbage and rusting parts from stolen vehicles stick out of the ground in an uncut, untended weed patch.

A tee shot has to carry 212 yards to get over the weed patch. If the player elects to lay up, he still has all of a 4-wood to the green. Even if his drive carries the weeds, the ground is almost always soggy near the weed patch, and you get no roll. It takes at least a 6-iron to carry onto a green protected by a pond filled with old motor oil, sludge and dead carp. Concentration is tough due to factory noise.

A great hole when the bets are all down and the press is on.

You're in jail on the tee at Leavenworth's No. 8
If there is one single hole that can take the heart out of you right away, it's in Leavenworth, Kan., at a public course. Much of the land in the area has been used for practice by Army engineers from nearby Fort Leavenworth, and the tee box on No. 8 is down in an immense hole. Grass will not grow in the hole, and if it rains, the mud doesn't dry for weeks. Leeches have made homes down there.

It's extremely humid in that part of Kansas in the summers, and there is no breeze whatsoever on the tee. A sewer runs nearby, and the smell is gamey, to say the least. The drive is almost 90 degrees straight up, and after you finally lug your clubs or pull your cart up the hill, the humidity leaves you completely soaked.

As you come to the crest of the hill, your first view is of the rat-gray stone of the Leavenworth Federal Penitentiary where, if there is any justice at all in this world, whoever designed that hole is doing 20 to life at this moment.

"Haaayy. You really let out the shaft on that one."

"He's an important client, Bascom, so I will shoot
in the mid-90's and you will have 104."

MY BUDDY, BYRON NELSON

by CHARLES BROME

Byron Nelson's path first crossed mine in a Portland, Ore., department store sometime during 1946, when he very graciously autographed my copy of "Winning Golf" by Byron Nelson.

After that I considered Byron Nelson a close personal friend, and I had his signature to prove it.

Our next actual meeting did not occur until recently, at a major golf tournament.

That encounter turned out to be a full-fledged, five-star, diamond-studded disaster. Two disasters, really. A major one the first day and a secondary eruption three days later.

This may very well puzzle you. How could a man as nice as Byron Nelson suddenly turn rotten and toss away a quarter of a century of friendship?

To understand, you must first appreciate just who Byron Nelson really is. You undoubtedly think of him as a pleasant, round-faced man on the TV set, wearing a funny little hat and adding a bit of weight here and there and putting up with a considerable amount of damned nonsense from the announcer. (That announcer INTERRUPTED Byron Nelson once. On his birthday, too. Byron Nelson just smiled and pretended not to notice.)

But that is only the Byron Nelson on TV. In real life, Byron Nelson is The Greatest Golfer in the World.

Ignorant people sometimes want to argue this point. They bring up names like Ben Hogan, or Jack Nicklaus, or lovable old Ken Waterman, but they're wrong.

ITEM. Byron Nelson, in 1945, won 11 PGA tournaments in succession. Not two or three. Eleven. Not 11 in a whole year. Eleven in a row. (He won 18 tournaments that year, for another all-time record, but I don't even bother to count that.)

ITEM. Byron Nelson's stroke average in 1945 tournament play was 68.33—nearly a full stroke lower than any Vardon Trophy winner has managed to achieve since.

ITEM. In the 1945 PGA, Byron Nelson allowed his attention to wander for a moment. The man is only human. The next thing you know, Mike Turnesa had him 2 down with four holes to go. (It was match play then.) Whereupon Byron Nelson shot birdie-birdie-eagle-par to win, 1 up.

ERGO. When somebody wins more than 11 tournaments in a row, averages fewer than 68.33 strokes for a year and has the presence of mind to finish birdie-birdie-eagle-par when he needs to, that person will then become The Greatest Golfer in the World and Byron Nelson can be thrown away.

Until that day, which there is a fat chance of anybody ever seeing, Byron Nelson is officially declared the greatest and I see no possible reason for discussing it further.

Starting about 1960 or so, I had more or less taken for granted that Byron Nelson had been put decently away in a museum. Stuffed and mounted and donated to Golf House, propped up in a glass case, probably.

To be sure, I had seen Byron Nelson on TV from time to time. But it certainly had never occurred to me that he might be real. After all, you see Heckle and Jeckle on TV, too, but you hardly expect to turn around on the first morning of a golf tournament and find them standing there so close you could reach out and erase them.

But that's what happened. I turned innocently around and there, not three feet away from me, stood Byron Nelson!

Alive. Breathing. I could hear him breathing. In and out.

Do you have the whole picture? The Greatest Golfer in the World had escaped from his glass case and was just sort of standing there like any ordinary person between seven and eight feet tall and in absolutely tip-top condition. (Byron Nelson looks great. Healthier than Gary Player. Not fat at all. It's those funny little hats that make him look that way. That and the fact that the announcer who interrupted Byron Nelson on his birthday is very skinny.)

To this day, I am not quite sure why the sight of Byron Nelson affected me the way it did, but the instant I saw him I came completely unstrung. Not gradually. Instantaneously. From recognition to shock to horror to blind panic to flight, in no seconds flat.

I ran. Byron Nelson was partially blocking the nearest escape route, and I actually had to push him aside to get by. I can still see the startled look on his face as he saw a grown man, apparently in the throes of some kind of seizure, lurch past him and go gibbering off into the distance.

That night in my motel room I was ready to pack up and go home. The chance of a lifetime to see a major golf tournament, and The Greatest Golfer in the World had spoiled it all! The man had no right to sneak out of his glass case and tiptoe up behind me like that.

But it hadn't really been Byron Nelson's fault and I knew it. As a matter of fact, he had actually provided me with an ideal opportunity to renew our friendship. I easily could have spoken to him.

"Byron Nelson, you are the greatest golfer in the world and I can prove it," I could have said. A man doesn't need the courage of a tiger to say that to somebody.

If it had been Ben Hogan, now, that would have been a different matter. "Mr. Hogan, I think you are the second-greatest golfer in the world, next to Byron Nelson, but I can't prove it." Nobody would blame himself for running away from that particular gambit.

I sat there in the dark, brooding, for a long time. My thoughts got blacker and blacker. Finally, of course, a light began to glimmer. I had behaved badly, very badly indeed. No doubt about that. But no matter how great the dishonor, was there not hope for redemption?

Yes! The next morning, I told myself—not the next afternoon, but the next morning—I would track down Byron Nelson. I would walk right up to him and I would look Byron Nelson straight in the eye and I would say firmly and distinctly, without clearing my throat first, "Byron Nelson, when I saw you yesterday I admit I was rattled, but I thought then and I think now that you are the greatest golfer in the world."

The more I thought about this, savored the words and visualized the scene, the better I felt. Walk right up to him and come out with it. Man to man.

Ten to one, I thought, a basically friendly man like Byron Nelson would sense that I was nervous, and he would say something helpful.

"Man cain't hep bein' scairt," he might say. (Byron Nelson is from Texas.)

And I would nod in agreement and maybe we would shake hands. No, *probably* we would shake hands. And I would mention to him that I still have my autographed copy of "Winning Golf." Upon hearing this, Byron Nelson would be very likely to look at me more closely, as if to confirm the first faint stirrings of recognition.

"What color of a fountain pen was it I used?"

"Light gray, very fat, and semi-filled with semi-permanent blue-black ink," I would instantly reply.

"What did I write?"

" 'Good luck,' " I would answer.

"Well cut off my laigs and call me Shorty!" he would burst out in his homespun Texas manner. "You must be Chuck Brome!"

"Guilty," I would say, with the sparkling wit that has made me famous. And we would both laugh and shake hands again, this time much more heartily.

"I like the cut of your jib, pardner," he would say, getting his Texas talk and his nautical talk mixed up for a minute.

And then, casually, as one golfer to another, "How you hittin' them?"

"Rotten," I would say.

(You must remember that this was all beginning to sound perfectly reasonable to me, sitting there in a dark motel room at two o'clock in the morning getting over being miserable. Nevertheless, the rules of my fantasy required that I maintain strict honesty about all matters of concrete fact.)

"Just rotten," I would admit. "I must have read "Winning Golf" and looked at the pictures a million times, but I still can't hit a ball 270 yards."

Byron Nelson would be genuinely surprised. "That's funny. I remember when I saw you in Portland that time I figured you for a man who would have one of the finest natural swings I ever saw."

And I would be forced by the rules to say that he must have been mistaken.

"Cain't be," he would frown. "Let's go out to the practice tee and have a look."

"There isn't any practice tee," I would say. "After I ran away from you yesterday I looked all over for it and there isn't any. These people are teeing off stone cold."

But Byron Nelson would just laugh and slap me on the back Texas-style, nearly breaking my shoulder, but I wouldn't mind, and his chauffeur-driven, air-conditioned limousine, upholstered in kangaroo hide, would appear, and we would get in and drive 30 to 40 miles to where the practice area was hidden.

When we got there we would get out and walk up to a large man with fairly tight pants and Byron Nelson would say, "Gimme your club."

"Yes, sir," Jack Nicklaus would say.

And I would swing the club (Jack Nicklaus' personal driver) a few times and pronounce it too heavy.

"You're right," Byron Nelson would say, looking hard at Jack Nicklaus, who would hang his head.

So we would go on down the line and come to a man with very broad shoulders and the second best disposition in the world, next to Byron Nelson's, and Byron Nelson would say, "Gimme your club."

"Yes, sir," Arnold Palmer would say.

But after swinging Arnold Palmer's club a few times I would find that it, too, was not properly weighted. So we would go still farther and finally come to a much smaller and grouchier person.

"Gimme your club," Byron Nelson would say.

"Yes, sir," Deane Beman would say.

And his club would feel fairly good except for a slightly too-stiff shaft and I would swing it a few times and then hit one of my better shots—100 yards in the general direction I intended and an additional 70 yards in a sickening curve off to the right where

Lee Trevino's caddie was catching 5-iron shots in his cap. Blindfolded.

I would look up at Byron Nelson apologetically. Deane Beman would look sick to his stomach. Lee Trevino's caddie would stuff the ball in his pocket.

But The Greatest Golfer in the World would whistle a long Texas whistle, because his eyes would have detected what no other eyes on earth were capable of detecting.

"Jest as I figgered," he would say. "Finest natural swing I ever saw in my life. Only one thing wrong, and it's my fault for not putting it in the book."

And he would reach into the pocket of his expensively tailored but not too tight pants and pull out a solid gold jackknife. Very carefully, he would cut a tiny, nearly invisible notch in the grip of Deane Beman's barely adequate driver.

"Put your left thumb smack into the top of that tiny, nearly invisible notch and hit another one," he would say quietly.

And I would do that several times and the ball would go 275 lovely yards down the exact center of the fairway, with either a perfectly controlled draw or fade at the end, depending on my whim of the moment, and Jack and Arnie and Lee would cheer.

"I feel rotten about leaving that part out of the book," Byron Nelson would say. "I wanted to put it in, but a man named Frank Hannigan of the U.S. Golf Association talked me out of it. Man with a mighty bad cut to his jib."

I would hasten to assure Byron Nelson that I didn't blame him.

"No," Byron Nelson would say, "I should have put it in. Man with a natural swing like yours could have made at least three million dollars on the tour. The next time I see Frank Hannigan, I will beat him up."

As we walked back to the car, we would turn and watch Deane Beman and Jack Nicklaus and Arnold Palmer and Lee Trevino and Lee Trevino's caddie taking turns hitting drives with their thumbs over the notch, but it didn't help them.

Byron Nelson would smile. "Only works with an absolutely perfect natural swing," he would say. "Those are all good boys, but they will never win more than three or four tournaments in a row. Five, tops."

On the drive back, I would be deep in thought. Byron Nelson would notice immediately.

"What's bitin' on you, pardner?" he would say. "Got a cut in your jib?"

And at first I would say it was nothing. But then I would realize that true friendship of the kind that existed between Byron Nelson and me demanded complete honesty, and I would tell him about my secret ambition—to be the first 50-year-old to win the Masters, the U.S. and British Amateurs, and the Lake Hopatcong Annual Catch-As-Catch-Can-and-Don't-Improve-Your-Lie-Unless-

You're-on-a-Really-Good-Sized-Rock Golf Tournament and Ice-Fishing Festival (Seniors Division), all in the same year.

"Tell me honestly, Byron Nelson, do you think if I got you to cut tiny, nearly invisible notches in the grips of all my clubs, I could achieve that ambition, modest though it may be?" I would ask.

And then it would be Byron Nelson's turn to be deep in thought. Finally he would say, "What kind of clubs you using now?"

(There in the motel room I winced when Byron Nelson asked me that, and I wished that I had not made the rules so inflexible. But there was no way out.)

I would be forced to confess that I use a set of Judy Kimball clubs because I have never in my life found a set of clubs that felt so lovely, but that I did wish the shafts were just a bit longer and the lies were just a shade less upright. And that I could figure out a way to file the "Judy Kimball" off them without messing up the balance, because some of the roughneck element at Lake Hopatcong are often less than gracious when they see that name.

I would add that I had never seen Judy Kimball, but that I hoped she was a big, husky woman and not some little shrimp of a girl.

And Byron Nelson, the finest friend a man ever had, would explain that Judy Kimball is six foot-four and weighs 235 pounds.

"Wrists and forearms on her like a lady gorilla," he would add comfortingly. "She once squeezed a man to death in Tulsa, Okla., just by shaking hands with him. Most men couldn't even lift a Judy Kimball club, let alone swing it."

And then he would look at me very carefully and would finally say, "Tell you what I'll do. I'll send you a brand-new set of Byron Nelson clubs, with exactly the same feel to them as the Judy Kimball clubs but with slightly longer shafts and slightly flatter lies. Each will be personally designed by me for your absolutely perfect natural swing. Each club will have a tiny, nearly invisible notch cut into the grip. And each club will last forever."

By now, Byron Nelson would be speaking with the voice of a prophet, saying, "Yea, and ye shall win the mighty victories of which ye spake. And it shall come to pass that in the final round of each tourney ye shall be paired with Jack, the mighty Nicklaus. And ye with yeer fine natural swing shall outdrive him by a good 30 yards every time, even though he practically gets a hernia trying to keep up with you, or ye, rather. And thenceforth he shall be termed by the writers of sports in the publick press not as the Golden Bear or anything like that, but as Pitty-Pat Jack."

And I would protest at first that he was doing too much for me, but eventually I would give in so as not to hurt his feelings.

"I get all that stuff free for wearing those funny little hats on the TV anyhow," he would explain. "Besides, I can't forgive myself for letting Frank Hannigan talk me out of putting the notches in the book, thus cheating you out of your well-deserved three million dollars." Byron Nelson would pound one enormous fist against the other thoughtfully, and I would feel a moment of pity for Frank Hannigan, despite his wickedness.

When we got back to the tournament, Byron Nelson would take me out to the TV tower, where we would throw the skinny announcer overboard and Byron Nelson and I would cover the rest of the tournament together.

"Never did like the cut of that man's jib," Byron Nelson would say. "He interrupted me once, you know. On my birthday."

Yes, I assured myself in groggy happiness, there in the motel room, it was going to be all right. The next morning, without fail, I would redeem myself.

To my credit, the next morning I really did try to find Byron Nelson. I looked everywhere. But he wasn't there.

On the third morning of the tournament he wasn't there either.

Nor on the fourth morning.

But late in the afternoon of the fourth day I saw him, standing in a crowd of inferior people.

I tried. God knows I tried. I had long since memorized my speech: "When-I-saw-you-the-other-day-I-admit-I-was-rattled, but-I-thought-then-and-I-think-now-that-you-are-the-greatest-golfer-in-the-world."

I said the words over and over as I inched my way toward him through the crowd.

Finally we were face to face. I don't think he recognized me when I was not having a seizure. At least he didn't turn pale.

I reached out compulsively and grabbed his hand, which was hanging at his side, in both of mine. I shook it as fast as I could. Up and down, up and down. It was horrible.

I even managed to get out part of my speech.

"I was rattled!" I said. I could hear myself saying it, but it was not my own voice. It was the voice of a woman in an advanced stage of hysteria. I tried again.

"I WAS RATTLED!" Louder this time, but in an even more insane soprano.

By now Byron Nelson was rattled, too. I don't blame him. But he was game. I want it clearly understood that The Greatest Golfer in the World, when confronted by a maniac, was game.

"Hi!" he said and managed a smile.

And I took off again.

"The word is 'nevermore,' not 'neverhappen.' "

"If there's anything to reincarnation, I hope I come
back as a New Rochelle housewife."

"What does he mean I'm getting to be a bore about my double-eagle?"

"Know what I think? I think Bert's trying
to break up the old foursome."

GOLF IS A TRIP

by JOHN UPDIKE

I have been asked to write about golf as a hobby. But of course golf is not a hobby. Hobbies take place in the cellar and smell of airplane glue. Nor is golf, though some men turn it into such, meant to be a profession or a pleasure. Indeed, few sights are more odious on the golf course than a sauntering, beered-up foursome obviously having a good time. Some golfers, we are told, enjoy the landscape; but properly the landscape shrivels and compresses into the grim, surrealistically vivid patch of grass directly under the golfer's eyes as he morosely walks toward where he thinks his ball might be. We should be conscious of no more grass, the old Scots adage goes, than will cover our own graves. If neither work nor play, if more pain than pleasure but not essentially either, what, then, can golf be? Luckily, a word newly coined rings on the blank Formica of the conundrum. Golf is a *trip*.

A non-chemical hallucinogen, golf breaks the human body into components so strangely elongated and so tenuously linked, yet with anxious little bunches of hyper-consciousness and undue effort bulging here and there, along with rotating blind patches and a sort of cartilaginous euphoria—golf so transforms one's somatic sense, in short, that truth itself seems about to break through the exacerbated and, as it were, debunked fabric of mundane reality.

An exceedingly small ball is placed a large distance from one's face, and a silver wand curiously warped at one end is placed in one's hands. Additionally, one's head is set a-flitting with a swarm of dimly remembered "tips." Tommy Armour says to hit the ball with the right hand. Ben Hogan says to push off with the right foot. Arnold Palmer says keep your head still. Arnold Palmer has painted hands in his golf book. Gary Player says don't lift the left heel. There is a white circle around his heel. Dick Aultman says keep everything square, even your right foot, to the line of flight. His book is full of beautiful pictures of straight lines lying along wrists like carpenter's rules on planed wood. Mindy Blake, in his golf book, says "Square-to-Square" is an evolutionary half-step on the way to a stance in which both feet are skewed toward the hole

66

and at the extremity of the backswing in the angle between the left arm and the line to the target is a mere 14 degrees. Not 15 degrees. Not 10 degrees. Fourteen degrees. Jack Nicklaus, who is a big man, says you should stand up to the ball the way you'd stand around doing nothing in particular. Hogan and Player, who are small men, show a lot of strenuous arrows generating terrific torque at the hips. Player says pass the right shoulder under the chin. Somebody else says count two knuckles on the left hand at address. Somebody else says no knuckle should show. Which is to say nothing about knees, open or closed clubface at top of backswing, passive right side, "sitting down" to the ball, looking at the ball with the right eye—all of which are crucial.

This unpleasant paragraph above, strange to say, got me so excited I had to rush out into the yard and hit a few shots, even though it was pitch dark, and only the daffodils showed. Golf converts oddly well into words. Wodehouse's golf stories delighted me years before I touched a club. The story of Jones' Grand Slam, and Vardon's triumph over J. H. Taylor at Muirfield in 1896, and Palmer's catching Mike Souchak at Cherry Hills in 1960, are always enthralling—as is, indeed, the anecdote of the most abject duffer. For example:

Once, my head buzzing with a mess of anatomical and aeronautical information that was not relating to the golf balls I was hitting, I went to a pro and had a lesson. Put your weight on the right foot, the man told me, and then the left. "That's all?" I asked. "That's all," he said. "What about the wrists pronating?" I asked. "What about the angle of shoulder-plane vis-a-vis that of hip-plane?" "Forget them," he said. Ironically, then, in order to demonstrate to him the folly of his command (much as the Six Hundred rode into the Valley of Death), I obeyed. The ball clicked into the air, soared straight as a string and fell in a distant ecstasy of backspin. For some weeks, harboring this absurd instruction, I went around golf courses like a giant, pounding out pars, humiliating my friends. But I never could identify with my new prowess; I couldn't internalize it. There was an immense semicircular area, transparent, mysterious, anesthetized, above the monotonous weight-shift of my feet. All richness had fled the game. So gradually I went back on my lessons, ignored my feet, made a number of other studied adjustments and restored my swing to its original, fascinating terribilità.

Like that golf story of mine? Let me tell you another: the greatest shot of my life. It was years ago, on a little dogleg left, downhill. Apple trees were in blossom. Or the maples were turning; I forget which. My drive was badly smothered, and after some painful, wounded bounces found rest in the deep rough at the crook of the dogleg. My second shot, a 9-iron too tensely gripped, moved a great deal of grass. The third shot, a smoother swing with the knees nicely flexed, nudged the ball a good six feet out onto the fairway. The lie was downhill. The distance to the green was perhaps 230 yards at this point. I chose (of course) a 3-wood. The lie was not only downhill but sidehill. I tried to remember some tip about sidehill lies; it was either (1) play the ball farther forward from the center of the stance, with the stance more open, or (2) play the ball farther back, off a closed stance, or (3) some combination. I compromised by swinging with locked elbows and looking up quickly to see how it turned out. A divot the size of an undershirt was taken some 18 inches behind the ball. The ball moved a few puzzled inches. Now here comes my great shot. Perfectly demented by frustration, I swung as if the club were an ax with which I was reducing an orange crate to kindling wood. Emitting a sucking, oval sound, the astounded ball, smitten, soared far up the fairway, curling toward the fat part of the green with just the daintiest trace of a fade, hit once on the fringe, kicked smartly toward the flagstick and stopped two feet from the cup. I sank the putt for what my partner justly termed a "remarkable 6."

In this mystical experience, some deep golf revelation was doubtless offered me, but I have never been able to grasp it, or to duplicate the shot. In fact, the only two golf tips I have found consistently useful are these. One (from Jack Nicklaus): on long putts, think of yourself putting the ball half the distance and having it roll the rest of the way. Two (from I forget—Mac Divot?): on chip shots, to keep from underhitting, imagine yourself throwing the ball to the green with the right hand.

Otherwise, though once in a while a 7-iron rips off the clubface with that pleasant tearing sound, as if pulling a zipper in space, and falls toward the hole like a raindrop down a well, or a drive draws sweetly with the bend of the fairway and disappears, still rolling, far beyond the applauding sprinkler, these things happen in spite of me, and not because of me. On the golf course as nowhere else, the tyranny of causality is suspended, and men are free.

DEAR SOPHIE: GOLF SCHOOL IS GREAT

by LARRY SHEEHAN

MONDAY EVE

Dear Sophie,

Well, the first day of golf school in sunny Florida is over and I am glad I enrolled, even though my hands are sore from hitting 1,372 range balls.

The pro for the school is Mr. Bob Toski himself. His book is the one on the table on my side of the bed next to the apple core and my 1957 edition of the Rules of Golf. Today in his introductory speech to all of us out on the practice tee he said he weighs 122 pounds, which is all you weighed when we got married. Then he hit 300-yard drives on one leg, on his knees, with one hand and with his eyes closed to show golf is a cinch.

The 36 of us are divided, like All of Gaul, into three groups according to handicap and naturally with my 24 I am in among the Visigoths, or Group C. We get both group and individual instruction much of the day, and the rest of the time we are free to hit balls or play one of the three grand Innisbrook layouts. Mr. Toski says that rather than try to rebuild our swings completely he will attack our worst tragedies and leave us with some answers.

According to the list passed out at the opening banquet, the people here are in upstanding lines such as law, land, medicine, business, industry and roller skating. There are 30 other men in the Golf Digest school, four women—all spoken for—and one youth who wishes to become another Bert Yancey. They range in age from 14 to 66, height from 5'1" to 6' 5", weight from 90 to 265 and handicap from 1 to 30.

Well, I hope I am not boring you with all these statistics. How are the kids and the dog and the winter?

Anyway, after I hit 1,372 balls, as I said, I played a round in the afternoon. I thought I would psych out my playing partners, Lewis and Gonzalo, by buying two packages of Titleists. But I lost five of the balls on the first two holes and that was embarrassing.

I played worse than Lewis, who has the highest handicap in the whole school with a 30. He has taken up golf to keep from going insane in his upcoming retired years.

This Gonzalo, believe it or not, came all the way from Venezuela for the school. We discussed the Incas and the Aztecs, naturally, and then I gave him tips on North American golfing customs, such as how to line up a putt in 10 minutes or more. I believe my friendliness paid off. For example, after I lost my five Titleists I asked him how to say "&@ℏ*!?*)&@" in Spanish and he was more than happy to tell me.

TUESDAY
Dear Sophie,

Today we were all lined up at our battle stations on the tee grooving our swings. Mr. Toski got to me at mid-morning and said, "Let's see what you can do."

So I took my broad-based subway riders stance and checked the V's in my grip to be sure my knuckles were white and then carved a swing arc in the shape of a coat hanger. I hit it fair.

Then Toski started tugging me around into new positions, he shook my hand like a limp noodle to give me an idea of grip pressure, he shouted advice about my posture.

Then he got behind me and grabbed my club with one hand and made me grab the club with one hand and we swung the club and the ball sailed over 200 yards! He threw his Ben Hogan cap in the air.

Then he smiled broadly and told me I wasn't listening well enough and hollered about my right side and said keep up the good work.

After he was gone, I drifted down the line and said, "Say, Lewis, where do I report assault and battery?"

But Lewis was talking to himself: "When I lighten my grip," he was muttering, "the weight of the clubhead will naturally cause my wrists to cock at the top of the backswing. . . ."

I walked down to Gonzalo and said "$*!&:ℏ@?*(&!"

But he was absorbed, too, saying in a mixture of Spanish and English something about how the way he turns his head away from the ball influences the shape of his swing plane and so he should learn to look sideways up the skirt of his target, so to speak, in the manner of J. Nicklaus.

I went back to my place. I narrowed my stance, lightened my grip and tried taking the club back in a lazier fashion as Toski had suggested. Once in a while there began to be a strange "click" in the sound of the shot instead of my usual "clunk."

WEDNESDAY
Dear Sophie,

I played golf with two Group B fellows from New York named Sal and Bernie, who have silver threads running through their apparel and stick together down here like spaghetti and meatballs.

Sal says he is target-conscious now and is setting up his club behind the ball before he sets his body. Bernie is working on trusting the sensation of his arms swinging down. They're already planning to go to the Doral next week with their new games.

I for one am having trouble. I don't care if there is a doctor here from Kentucky who is at his third school in three years. I wish I was home with the kids and the dog. How could I leave them for golf?

THURSDAY EVE
Dear Sophie,

I was just aiming wrong. In two minutes this morning Mr. Toski straightened out the whole mess, can you imagine? First, he made me line up, then he got into my exact stance himself and had me take a look at it from behind the ball, and sure enough I had the old Howitzer aiming 50 yards left of target. Misalignment is a common tragedy, he said, and he collected all of us with common alignment problems and gave us a 30-minute special clinic. When you are aligned poorly, your unconscious starts fiddling with your swing plane. I am not a great believer in the unconscious, of course, or in weird ideas in general, but this is a free country and the important thing is I'm suddenly clicking two shots out of every five.

I mingled with the top players in Group A, who are seething with determination. Why, there are four low-handicappers who came down here together from Michigan and they have been tape-recording and filming each other and their lessons every step of the way. One of them says he is enjoying fleeting moments of greatness on the golf course and wishes to give up his sideline as a heart surgeon.

There is a Virginian here with a 1 handicap. He says he is at the school to get himself more length so he can handle the young whippersnappers he plays against in various summer tournaments.

At dinner as usual we sit around in various groups regaling each other with golf talk.

Sal and Bernie told how they had gone to Pinehurst with two cronies for a week of golf once and then came back in the middle of the week in four separate planes because of a disputed out-of-bounds call.

Gonzalo said he was learning how to swear in English.

The wife of a pickle manufacturer told how it is impossible to be both husband and golf instructor to the same individual, meaning herself, and how she loves Mr. Toski's enthusiasm. He barely takes time for lunch.

The president of six corporations recommended jogging.

A man from Group A said that now that he had gotten his swing straightened out he was going to enroll in Masters and Johnson next.

We are a close-knit group, reminiscent of Basic Training, and the food is even better.

FRIDAY (LATE)
Dear Sophie,

First off I should not have gone jogging with the magnate. We ran for 20 minutes on the dewy fairways listening to remedies for hiccups on the transistor radio. I had to go back to bed after.

Second of all, I did not get my own personal cassette tape lesson dictated by Mr. Toski, a highlight of the school. Here is what happened. I was at the end of the tee. Mr. Toski got to the wife of the pickle manufacturer who was second to last, and in the course of giving her the final poop, he got excited and started talking to the world at large.

Well, before too long a mass of humans gathered, including tennis players, retired folk, landscapers, the mailman and a telephone repair crew. Pretty soon my position on the tee was overflowing.

Mr. Toski then demonstrated how Smith College girls used to swing, gave a history of the game, performed trick shots and recalled his tournament playing days. After 40 minutes he stopped and the 135 spectators departed along with him and the tape recorder, leaving me fondling my 4-wood on the broad empty tee.

So that is why I had too much to drink at the wind-up cocktail party for the school this evening and why, when I went around toasting everyone's new golf swing, it was with a heavy heart.

SATURDAY AFTERNOON
Dear Sophie,

This morning at the school finale Mr. Toski gave a clinic on sand shots and one on putting for all 36 of us and everyone gasped and clapped and took notes.

Naturally, I was not going to say anything about missing my cassette tape even though I felt like I had just gone through four years of college and not gotten my diploma.

Then at the end of the clinic Mr. Toski called me over and said it was time for my cassette tape lesson. How is that for a true gentleman!!?! He took me to one side and talked into the recorder and reviewed all the work we had done on my swing and told me exactly how I should practice to get to be a clicker more of the time instead of a clunker. He said I should master my game from green to tee instead of from tee to green and that I should begin by working on my stroke for six-inch putts.

But you can hear the tape yourself when I get home, which will be a few days later than I had originally planned since it is so nice and warm down here, and as Sal and Bernie point out, I might as well work on my game while I have the golden opportunity.

How are the kids and the dog?

"OK. You can knock off the goofy practice swing.
I got us four a side!"

HOW I HUSTLED $180,000 IN A WEEK OF GOLF

by BOBBY RIGGS

Golf opened up a whole new world to me. I took up the game during the wave of prosperity right after World War II when people had plenty of time to spend on the course and plenty of money to bet on themselves.

At the La Gorce Country Club in Miami Beach, I saw ordinary golfers shooting 85 and 90 and betting all kinds of money. I asked myself, "How long has this been going on?" I went out on the course and took a few shots off the first tee. I figured that anybody who was any kind of athlete at all should have no trouble playing this game. Without taking a lesson, but watching good players carefully, I was soon breaking 100 consistently. It wasn't long before I was shooting in the 80's. In my first year at the game I got my handicap down to 16.

Golf lends itself so beautifully to betting because of this handicapping system. According to official rules, a handicap is determined by the average score of a player's most recent rounds. But in most "friendly" betting, handicaps are worked out on the first tee after a lot of arguing and negotiating. I always enjoyed negotiating as much as I did the golf itself. Someone once said, "Golf matches are not won on the fairways or the greens; they are won on the tee—the first tee." Somebody else also said, "The second worst thing in the world is betting on a golf game and losing. The worst is not betting at all." I've never agreed with any philosophy more.

I soon discovered that my lifelong competitive background in tennis was a tremendous plus factor on the golf course. If I played a businessman on vacation who had the same handicap as mine, he would fall apart when the going got tough. He would start slicing, shanking, making mistakes of all kinds, as soon as we had a little bet going. I always thrived under pressure in tennis and the same thing held true in golf, particularly when the money was down.

People called me a hustler and a thief when I was shooting to a 10 handicap: "That son of a gun should be a 6 or 8 handicap." That wasn't true. I really was a legitimate 10. But I had intangibles that made me better than another 10. This held true all the way down, as I improved and my handicap dropped to three, which was as low as it ever got—meaning that I consistently shot in the 70's.

I never took any lessons, just played along with good players—occasionally with someone like Sam Snead—and watched how they did it.

Life Magazine was responsible for giving me a false reputation back in those days, one that has stayed with me. In an article entitled "Larceny on the Links" the magazine ran my picture along with those of the big hustlers of the time—John Montague, Titanic Thompson and others. They were the real thing, authentic hustlers, but I didn't belong in that company. I didn't play that well. Besides I never falsified my handicap as most hustlers will, if given the opportunity. The only reason Life included me in the list was that I was a well-known figure in another sport who had turned to golf with some success.

The magazine did quote me correctly as stating that "golf courses today are just big, open-air poolrooms," and warning unsuspecting golfers from betting with strangers on the course.

The characters involved in golf hustling were a colorful lot, and I played against some of them in the early days of my own golf career. Martin Stanovich, better known as The Fat Man, was an overweight, awkward guy, who straddled the ball and gave the impression that he was nothing but a hacker. This was a fateful mistake that many of his opponents made.

"Look at that guy," Lee Trevino once said. "You'd say he couldn't beat his way out of a paper pag. But he'll 68 you to death —a hell of a player."

Titanic Thompson, who was in his 70's when I first saw him in action, was a lean, tall guy who had a bagful of tricks as well as clubs. One of his favorite stunts was to play somebody right-handed, lose the round and then offer to play left-handed if he got a generous handicap. The stakes would increase to $5,000 or $10,000 and Titanic would win—because he was a natural southpaw.

Titanic would bet you $10,000 he could hit a golf ball a mile. Then he'd take you to the top of Pike's Peak and slam the ball downhill. Or he'd take you to a frozen lake in the wintertime and hit the ball across the ice—it would never stop.

When age began to catch up with him, Titanic collected a stable of young unknown players who shot better-than-average golf. He took them on tour and matched them against established players for big stakes.

The rough was full of colorful characters, all looking for action in the early 1950's. There was the Wiggler, Shaggy Ralph, the Dog Man, Charlie the Blade, Three-Iron Ward, the Fireman, Sneezy and the Whisky Drinker, The Stork and the Invalid. There was also supposed to be a strawberry-blonde lady hustler but I never caught up with her. This was long before the days of Women's Lib, and the golf courses I played were a male monopoly.

Charlie the Blade used only one club, a 4-iron, but he could do as much with it as most pros using all 14 clubs.

The Stork's gimmick was to play every shot off his right foot with the left stuck up behind him. He could shoot a 71 that way, too. The Invalid complained loudly about his aching back, but always managed to beat his handicap.

The Whisky Drinker carried a flask around the course with him. I suspected that the flask contained nothing stronger than tea, but he started nipping on the first hole and by the time he reached the ninth tee he was lurching and "tipsy." He would demand loudly that all bets be doubled—then sober up on the back nine and take all the dough.

I saw or played against this ragtag gang but I never met the legendary Mystery Man, John Montague, who earned his reputation in California. He could blast a buried ball out of a sand trap with a wooden club. He had all kinds of stunts. In a motel room he would open the window six inches and chip balls through the opening time after time without breaking the glass.

But, Life Magazine to the contrary, I was never in a class with these authentic hustlers. I never falsified my handicap. This is the cardinal sin in golf and one that eventually produced a major scandal.

This occurred during a Calcutta handicap match at the Deepdale Country Club on Long Island in 1955. I played in the match but knew nothing about the two golfers from New Jersey who won it.

Calcutta pools were declared illegal by the U.S. Golf Ass'n after what happened at Deepdale. Calcutta pools ran as high as $250,000 in those days. The one at Deepdale was a comparatively modest $45,000 affair. In a Calcutta teams were auctioned off to bidders, usually club members, for prices based on players' declared handicaps. The two New Jersey golfers listed handicaps of 17 and 18, and bought tickets on themselves. Actually their handicaps were 3. So they had no trouble at all winning for a prize of $16,000. Someone in the crowd who knew their real handicaps recognized them and complained to the officials after they had left with the money. In the resulting hue and cry Calcuttas were outlawed by all golf clubs. The incident alerted the golf public to the activities of hustlers and put most of them out of business.

Golf is a far better betting game than tennis, which is one reason I was so intrigued by it. You can handicap tennis in a lot of weird ways, but in golf everybody handicaps the same way, by strokes.

There are a thousand and one ways of betting on golf—and I've tried them all.

The standard bet is the Nassau. In $50 Nassaus, which were

commonplace in Florida in those days, you bet $50 on the first nine, $50 on the second nine and $50 on the 18—for a total Nassau of $150. They tell me the average Nassau now is $2, which shows you what's happened in this country since those free-spending days.

In those days in Florida the money seemed to grow on the palm trees. People were playing golf every day—and playing the stock market over the phone. There were a lot of "regulars" betting $1,000 Nassaus or more. They were oil millionaires from Texas and people who had cleaned up in real estate or stocks. They had money and didn't mind betting it.

Since I took up golf so late in life, I never developed a really good, grooved swing. I was not a long driver—225 or 230 yards or so off the tee. But I did learn to play well around the greens. I had "touch" with a golf club, just as I had with a tennis racquet. I was good at chipping—using a sand wedge that Sam Snead gave me when I first started—and became a first-class putter. I was so good that sometimes tournament players such as Gary Player and Bruce Crampton asked me how I did it. My answer probably puzzled them: "I just stare at the hole—I concentrate on getting the ball in the hole. I don't know how I do it—but it just goes in."

Down in Miami Beach I'd often play a round of golf with a half dozen bets going with bookmakers who followed me around the course. These guys would try to distract me when I was about to make a shot. Just as I leaned over the ball they'd crash two golf carts together. They'd move around me on the tee or green to disturb me. But I knew what they were up to and I never let them bother me.

These sharpies would also get to the caddies. If I asked my caddie on the putting green, "How do you think the ball will break —right or left?" the kid would be paid off to give the wrong reading. You could never make a six-foot putt. The kid would say, "It breaks sharply to the left," so you putt to the right of the hole and the ball breaks right, missing the hole by a mile.

The caddies would also "wrong club" you when they were paid off—advising you to use a 7-iron when the distance from the green really called for a 5-iron, so that you'd end up short, even if you made a good shot.

Some of the guys I bet with went around and changed the course on me. They liked to bet me that I couldn't break 80. At the time I was just about an 80 shooter. But they'd say, "You've got to play from the back of the tees." They'd get up at the crack of dawn, go to the greenkeeper, and give him $20 to put all the pins in the toughest places on the greens, as they do for the touring pros. It was pretty hard to take the bookies' money.

There was one fellow who liked to bet that I couldn't break 40 on a given nine holes. He'd walk along with me when I was playing in a foursome. He would bet me $500 that I could not break 40 in the first nine. I'd score 38 or 39. He wouldn't bet on the second nine—and I'd take a 41 or more. The next round he'd lay off the first nine and I'd be over 40. He'd come in with a bet on the second nine and I'd shoot 38. It was uncanny. He never guessed the right nine. I must have won 10 bets in a row from him.

Another bookmaker liked to go round with Marty Stanovich, the Fat Man, and bet with him. One time I was in a foursome playing against the Fat Man and the Fireman. Marty hooked his drive on the first hole, went out-of-bounds and ended up with a 7. He hooked again off the second tee and finished the hole with a 6. The bookmaker then offered to bet Marty $5,000 that he couldn't break 70 on the round. Although he was already 4 over par on the first two holes, the Fat Man took the bet.

The Fat Man then proceeded to score eight successive 3's—and the sequence included a par-5 hole and three par 4's—and finished his round with 69. He won the $5,000 and also killed us in our Nassau. It was the greatest exhibition I've ever seen. The Fat Man was always at his best when the big chips were down.

Playing with the Fat Man was good for my game, because I was always under pressure. I was playing a lot by this time at Plandome Golf Club, near my home on Long Island.

My best scores came when there was considerable money riding on the matches. One day at Plandome I went around the course with a member I'd often played with before. We had a $100 Nassau going on the round and I won the first 18. We played a second round, with "presses" on each nine—doubling the bet—and I won that, too. My opponent was desperate to get even, so he insisted on a third round. By this time I was getting into a groove and the course was as familiar to me as my own back yard. I ended up scoring a 66—my all-time best. But that was the only satisfaction I got. My opponent's check for $5,400 bounced, he dropped out of the club and I never got paid off.

The most successful match I ever played was in 1969 at the Concord Hotel in the Catskills on a course that is well-named—the Monster. I'd been having a series of matches with this individual and I always gave him a handicap. We had never seen the Monster before and it turned out to be one of the longest and most difficult courses I've ever played.

We had 10 different Nassaus going all at once. I was playing him even, giving him one shot, giving him two shots, and 3, 4, 5, 6, 7, 8 and 9 shots. Every match was played four ways—the front nine; the back nine twice and the 18. In addition, we had automatic presses on all the bets. This is what I call action.

When the smoke cleared that day, I had beaten my opponent 52 different ways. The stakes were $100 a bet so I ended up with $5,200 on the 18 holes.

By all odds the most action I ever got on the golf course was at The Greenbrier in White Sulphur Springs, W. Va., playing an oilman from Indiana. This was a year or so after I had taken up golf.

I'd played this millionaire earlier that year in Florida and we ended up about even in the betting. He had not been playing much so he worked out a bet with me that would have been good for him if he'd been playing as well as he had in Florida earlier in the year.

I gave him a stroke on every hole but the par 3's. We started out playing a $1,000 Nassau. He started so badly on the front nine that he wanted to press when he got two holes down and make a fresh bet. He lost each press. When it was all over that first day he had lost about $10,000.

The next day he wanted to raise the stakes. Since I was now playing on his money, I had nothing to lose and I said OK. But I had to give him a stroke on every hole, including the par 3's. It didn't make any difference, he played so badly. He blew up from his regular 100 game to about 135. I was still shooting my regular 85. So he ended the second day $20,000 down to me. By the time the week was over, although I kept increasing his handicap, he had lost $180,000. He also lost another bundle to a baseball owner who was in our foursome.

But there is a sequel to the story. A few weeks later in New York, the oilman invited me to a suite in the Sherry Netherland Hotel where he had organized a gin rummy game. My poor luck with cards was running as usual. So the oilman, an excellent gin player, took most of my golf winnings away from me in a couple of sessions at cards.

Once I was in a foursome at the Greenacres Country Club in Trenton, N.J., playing a big Nassau. About $1,000 was going to change hands. My partner had to go home after the first 18, so I continued the match alone, playing two balls against the other pair and taking the score of my best ball. In other words, I had myself for a partner. I liked to play that way. Some people would get tired playing two balls around a course, but I could do it all day long.

Coming into the 18th green there was quite a bit of money swinging on the match. It was a par-5 hole and both of my opponents were on the green in three. I hit a poor approach shot and landed short of the green in three. I took out the wedge that Sam Snead gave me and pitched the ball into the hole for a birdie 4. My opponents were so startled that both missed their birdie putts and I won the hole.

We wanted to play a third round but it was getting dark by then. So we played only the final three holes.

At the 18th the same situation developed again. My opponents were on the green in three and I was short of the green. As I took out my wedge I said, "Wouldn't it be funny if lightning struck again?" "Oh, go on and shoot," one of them yelled.

I swung the wedge, the ball landed in front of the hole and rolled into the cup for a birdie 4. The two guys missed their birdie putts and I took all the money. That was the last time I played golf.

"Let's not overdo the good loser bit, Harold."

"If they don't show up in the next 10 minutes
we tee off without 'em."

THE FOREST LAKERS' BIG DAY AT THE MASTERS

by WILLIAM PRICE FOX

Every April, every year, loaded down with golf shoes, umbrellas, fried chicken, barbecue, a guitar-saxophone-and-trumpet trio and a bonded-not-to-drink driver, a bus load of Forest Lake members makes its pilgrimage to the Masters. It's a short trip, only 60 miles from Columbia, S.C., and can be driven in an hour.

The Forest Lakers, a blue-blazered, red-faced group reminiscent of English hunting scenes, permit no wives, mothers, daughters, small sons or girlfriends. A few of the higher handicappers have been known to take an occasional sherry before dinner.

While the members can afford to charter a bus, hire a driver and buy all the barbecue they can carry, money won't touch Melvin Hemphill. Melvin, the pro at Forest Lake and the saxophonist for the trio, said he wasn't going. The word was out that if Fritz Vogel came along Melvin was staying home. He would rather watch it on television.

A month before, Fritz Vogel, handicap 22, had signed up for 24 hours of Melvin's lessons. Fritz had never broken 90. After six hours on the practice tee with Fritz, Melvin began losing weight. He couldn't sleep, his hands began to itch. He began drinking his bourbon straight and jiggling 10-grain blue Valiums in his pocket. "I just can't stand watching him swing. I almost get sick. How am I going to teach him anything?"

Fritz Vogel's three-piece swing was a nightmare ending with a vicious, snapped-off follow-through and two quick left steps sideways to keep from falling down. "It's like he's swinging a live eel. Isn't there some way we can keep him off the course? Tennis? Bowling? Somebody get him a woman."

"He's got Ethel."

"That's what I mean."

To discourage Vogel, Melvin sold him new clubs, new shoes, a new wardrobe. He changed his grip, his stance, his turn. Everything. Nothing worked. Fritz's needle was on 94-96 as if it were painted there. But Fritz wouldn't give up. By day he practiced and played. By night he read. He read Tom Morris The Elder's "Recollections of Carnoustie," Casper's "Philosophy," Yancey's "Testimonials" and Poindexter's "Golf in Depth."

After his rounds Fritz cornered Melvin behind the counter in the pro shop. "Listen to this," he said as he spread his scorecard out. There were arrows, crosses, circles, diagrams of shots and traps and tiny sketches of trees. Footnotes to the game.

"OK, on the first tee I hit a drive up the left side. It stopped out about 180, maybe 185, right under the pine. Melvin, I was thinking about fading a 4-iron up short and. . . ."

Melvin listened to the shot-by-shot account of the first hole. Fritz then led him down the graveled walk to the second tee. Melvin was trapped, there was no way out. Fritz unwrapped a ham sandwich and opened a pint of milk. "Melvin, this wood shot was low. Low. Quail high. It took off like one of Hogan's old babies . . . I think I know what I was doing there." He touched Melvin's sleeve. "Did you ever read Poindexter?" Melvin knew enough to say no to everything. "No."

To avoid the post-mortems Melvin tried eating lunch in the dining room. But here Fritz calmly slipped off his spikes and padded across the hardwood floor in his socks. "Melvin, you won't believe what happened out there today."

"You break 90?"

"Fifty going out, 46 coming in. It should have been an easy 84." He ordered a drink, soup, a sandwich and told the waiter they were not to be disturbed. He smoothed his card out and cleared his throat. "OK, on the first tee I said to myself, Fritz old boy, this time you're going to do it right."

Melvin could feel the warm exhaustion washing over him. Panic fluttered like a trapped bat. He was thinking about other careers, other parts of the country. He also knew that wild horses and locomotives would never drag him over to the nightmare at the Masters.

But two of the members had a desperate plan to keep Fritz off the bus. They invited Ethel to come along and she accepted. It was the morning of departure and Fritz and Ethel sat in the corner at the club away from the Bloody Marys and the salty jokes. Fritz's face was grim, dark. Ethel was the only woman in the room. Donald Dunlap was giggling like a schoolboy and nudging Melvin. "I knew it would work. I knew it. Pro, you coming along?"

Melvin smiled, "Damn right."

Out on the highway Bloody Marys and screwdrivers were being mixed and poured and Melvin was leading the trio into "Blue Skies." The driver checked his rear-view mirror and motioned back. Fritz's car was following. Ethel was driving. She was pulling up close. The bus slowed and Fritz leaned out the window, shouting through the slipstream: "I want in on the calcutta."

Donald leaned down. "Who do you want?"

"Weiskopf for a hundred! And give me the field."

Donald shouted over the diesel noise: "We're splitting it in half. Top or bottom?"

"Bottom for another hundred."

The calcutta went fast. Nicklaus sold for $250. Green and Miller $150 each. Melvin and Donald then readjusted the names for a new bottom of the field and waved Fritz up for the news. The road cleared and Ethel eased up. Fritz's head came out of the window, "How'd I do?"

"You got Weiskopf for $100."

"Terrific! How about the field?"

"It took another hundred."

Fritz checked up on the road. Then he cupped his hands. "Who's in it?"

"Well, it's . . . it's." Donald had to pull back. He was laughing so hard he couldn't talk. He wiped his eyes. "I can't do it. I can't."

Melvin said, "Let me. I got to see his face."

Donald recovered. "No, this one's mine."

The members jammed the windows, waiting, watching.

Donald leaned back out. "Bad news, Fritz."

"Well, who the hell's in it?"

"Gene Sarazen and Ralph Guldahl." Both were no longer serious contenders and only played for old times' sake.

Fritz screamed: "God All Mighty!"

Ethel had to drop back for another car. When she pulled up again Donald had closed the windows and drawn the shades. Fritz was pounding on the horn but now no one was listening. The trio was playing "Georgia on My Mind." A Coleman unit was keeping the barbecue hot and a portable refrigerator was clicking off the ice cubes. Everyone was drinking. Everyone was singing.

Nearing the Savannah River, the Jesus Saves and She-Crab-Soup signs were thickening up. Crossing the river the big green sign announced, "WELCOME TO GEORGIA—HOME OF THE MASTERS." A motorcycle escort met them at the Welcome Center and 10 minutes later they were cruising up one side of Broad Street and down the other serenading the bewildered Augustans with "Carolina in the Morning." The next stop was the parking lot.

Melvin and Donald went out on the course where they could see the shots on the 12th and the 13th. Ethel and Fritz, with a cooler of food, had followed them out. Tennessee Ernie Ford, in the shade of the big pine tree where he stays every year, was focusing his binoculars on the 13th tee. "Arnie's hitting! Here it comes!"

Palmer pushed a long fade toward the trees near them and he started for it. Tennessee Ernie sang out: "Here comes the King! And don't y'all be forgetting it!"

The crowd formed a ring around the ball tight enough to read the compression. Fritz and Ethel closed in with them. Palmer came down the slot. Ethel moved in, sighing, once high, once low.

"Lordy! Look how they crowd round that teeny ball. It's like an accident. Like somebody was hurt."

As Palmer approached his ball he saw Melvin. "Hello, Melvin."

"Hey, Arnie."

Gary Player was away and Palmer waited, hitching up his pants. "You staying through Sunday?" An official was pushing the crowd back.

"I'm going to try."

Then Melvin realized that Fritz was humming a single note in his ear.

"Mmmmmmm. If I could just shake his hand. That's all. Just shake his hand. Melvin, could you . . .?"

"Not now, Fritz."

Ethel moved in. "Mr. Palmer, would you like a nice egg salad sandwich? It's fresh."

Palmer grinned. "Yes ma'am. I haven't eaten all day. I just can't go that barbecue." The caddie held the sandwich while Arnie hit. The ball went stiff for the pin. "Thank you ma'am. See you, Melvin."

"Take care, Arnie, and good luck."

Ethel was beaming. "Oh, he's so cute. He's like some farm kid that just jumped off a truck. No wonder the little girls love him so."

Melvin knew he had to get away from them. He would wait and watch Nicklaus' shot, then he would vanish. But Fritz had slid in closer. "You know what's wrong with Palmer's swing?" He didn't wait for an answer. "He swings too hard for his body type. He can't finish high enough. Now you take my swing. Of course I don't swing nearly as hard as Arnie but I swear if I don't finish it higher. . . ."

And then Melvin realized something. Fritz was like Muzak. You tapped your foot to it. You hummed along with a refrain but you never actually listened to it. It was like the air-conditioner hum and the pine smell of a room spray. It wasn't meant to be paid attention to. Fritz was droning on about Palmer, Miller, Player. All were rolled into one big problem. "You take those swings and you examine them close. They're all flawed. Seriously flawed. Oh, I'd give anything if Poindexter could have lived to see this." Ethel stood at his side, nodding, agreeing. It was a marriage made in heaven.

Nicklaus was approaching his ball and Fritz wrapped his arm around her waist. "It's Nicklaus, honey. We call him The Golden Bear. Watch him now, he's the greatest of the great." Suddenly Fritz grabbed Melvin's arm. "Hey! He's got a five! Melvin, see that wind! It's a 4-iron."

It was too much for Melvin. "Fritz! For Christ's sake! Shut up!"

"But it's the wrong club. He can't get there with it."

Ethel said, "Well, tell him."

"Who?"

"Nicklaus."

"You can't do that."

"Well, I can." Suddenly she waved and shouted, "Hey Jack! Jack Nicklaus! Four-Iron! It's a 4-iron!"

An official rushed over. "Lady, for God's sake!"

Melvin was ducking into his dark glasses, pretending he was someone else. Nicklaus addressed the ball again. He hit. He was short. He started over. From a distance he looked mad. And then he saw Melvin. "That you, Melvin?"

"Hello, Jack."

He came over. "This lady with you?"

"Sorry about that."

"It's OK. I should have listened."

Melvin introduced them.

When Ethel shook his hand she held on. "It was Fritz's idea, not mine. You want to know what he says about your swing?"

Nicklaus looked at Melvin, faintly smiling, faintly frowning. "You sure you want to tell me?"

"Well, Melvin Hemphill here won't do it unless he charges you an arm and a leg and sells you a $400 golf bag. My Fritz here says you've got a flawed swing. It's your right elbow. It does something wrong."

Ethel crossed her arms and took a deep breath. "Well now, I've said it and I'm glad I got it over with."

Nicklaus nodded. "Thanks. It'll give me something to think about." He watched Melvin pulling his cap bill low. "You sending me a bill, pro?"

Fritz laughed quickly to get his attention. Then he made his move. "Jack. You don't mind if I call you Jack. I've been following you since '61. Every year. I'm right here. Same spot. Same station. Let me ask you something personal. You ever read Poindexter's "Golf In Depth"?

"Afraid not."

"Well, Jack, that book has turned my game completely around. I had this problem of a fast backswing and. . . ."

But Nicklaus, who had been playing from the back tees since he was 14, saw it coming. He had seen it before and knew it. It was in the dark conspiracy of the eyebrows, the thrust of the jaw and the crazy shine in the eyes. It was in the sly way Fritz hushed his voice to a whisper and then oozed forward as if he were going to pounce. Fritz was in close. He was more than a fan, more than an acquaintance. He was a friend. A buddy. He took Jack's elbow. But Nicklaus was backing away. "Fritz, I'd sure like to hear about it. Maybe now isn't the right time."

"I understand. Don't worry about it." Fritz's eyes narrowed wisely. "I'll send it to you. No trouble at all."

Nicklaus said, "Thanks, Fritz."

He hooked his head and pointed his finger. "Right-o, Jack."

Nicklaus said, "See you, Melvin."

"OK, Jack. Good luck."

He moved down the fairway and Ethel sang out: "God bless you, Jack Nicklaus! You go win this thing now, hear?"

Nicklaus waved. "I'm going to try," he said.

The day was over and Melvin headed back across the course for the parking lot. The members were counted, recounted. No one was missing and the long bus pulled out, heading away from the setting sun. Drinks were being mixed and sandwiches were being unwrapped. Someone was complaining, "Man, I can't go that cold barbecue. What happened to those pimento cheeses?"

"Gone. Here's some chicken left. Hey, Melvin, how about playing something? This bunch is dragging."

Melvin opened his case and called down the aisle, "Any requests?"

"Rambling Rose . . . Mona Lisa . . . Send in the Clowns."

He tightened his mouthpiece and adjusted the reed. "Let's do all three. Somebody knock me down with a bourbon. OK, men. A-one-and-a-two-and-a-three. . . ."

They played three sets before the requests ran out. The members were tired. Donald was asleep. Someone was snoring. Melvin broke his saxophone down and snapped it in the case. He moved across the driver. He wanted to be alone. He wanted to think. It was getting darker now and the red and blue neon was twinkling along the road. Like the members he, too, was weary. Too much sun. Too much Georgia.

Too much Fritz. He watched the white line and the honky-tonk neon and tried to read the church scriptures, hoping for some message. He was planning Fritz's next lesson. It was going to be the last. It would be simple. He would do it straightforward and fast and get it over with. He would say, "Sorry, Fritz. The lessons are over. I'll give you a refund. You can take cash or equipment." Or maybe, "Fritz, you won't believe this but my doctor said I had to start taking it easy and recommended that. . . ."

But as he saw the green dome of the Capitol shining in the distance and the lights of Columbia reflecting in the clouds, a drearier thought rose behind his eyes and darkened his mood. He knew, as he had always known, that for every 10 golfers who played first-flight golf there were a hundred Fritz Vogels. Like the brown sparrow, dusty and songless, they were everywhere. Everywhere.

Doomed forever to be an embarrassment on the first tee, they would go shanking, skulling and smother-hooking down the fairways of the world. And with all their lessons, their literature, their new equipment and their never-ending plumb-bobbing it would always be 105—106—107. Yes, they would win the wilder-carded Scotch foursomes. Yes, they would skull a 7-iron through the traps and up for a closest-to-the-pin award. And, yes, they might one day break 100 from the middle tees. Then maybe on some spectacular day their 89 minus their 22 for a net 67 would send them home with the mantlepiece trophy for their kids and friends, who didn't know gross from net, and their lives might very well be complete.

Yes, it was a mystery. No, he would never understand it. And, yes, the next lesson would be like the last and the lesson before that.

"OK, Fritz, let's hit a few and we'll see what you're doing. That's it. Thatta boy."

"Let's firm up that grip."

MUNY GOLF
TAKES GUTS

by JAY CRONLEY

I requested a tee-off time at 10 a.m. on a Saturday that was
promised lovely—temperature between 70 and 80 and a fast track.
Wind: none. Moisture: in Coors cans.

"No."

Well, yes, I see. Let's make it 9 a.m. Should be able to shake it
up by then.

"No. Full."

Eight? No. Seven? No. Noon? No way. One? Ha-ha. Two? You
a comedian? Three, four, five p.m.? Three noes. Six a.m.? Out of
the question. When then? Which is where 5:30 a.m. comes in.

It comes in quickly. It is not completely light at 5:30 a.m. It is
not anything, except mighty still—still dark, still before the
newspaper, still stiff. Any false hopes you had about feeling
heavenly vanishes between squints. If you are not the son or
daughter of the pro, chef, parking lot guy, mayor or keeper of the
greens, you are out of luck, Mac. Municipal players are best
characterized as Macs.

We drink beer, clonk around in any number of stripes and
dots, stand in line and get wicked sunburns.

Don't feel all that sorry for us. We get to play golf without
shirts. The men. We can find from one to 20 golf balls per 18-hole
round. The country club player pays for the right to shoot a quick,
comfortable, fashionable 90. We do it furiously, for maybe $10
total, if we get the bounce.

There are those who have never played a municipal golf
course, the Esquires and III's and Van-Somethings, and it is to them
that I dedicate this material. While you are scratching your toes on
rich carpet in the men's lounge, we are trying to hit an 8-iron off
bare dirt that is nourished only by spilled pop.

Now, I have played some splendid municipal courses, one in
Albuquerque with fairway grass as thick as welcome rugs, and one
in Ireland that played through castle ruins. The difference then is
psychological. You must summon inner courage to tee it up with a
man dressed in sneakers, an ascot and a glove on the wrong hand,

who says, "Mind if I play through?" on the No. 1 tee.

I find a particular thrill in standing on the putting green and being watered down by an attendant in a plantation hat who "speek no Eenglish, Meester."

It is my contention that anybody, with proper money, can play a country club golf course. It requires I'll-lead-us-to-Omaha-Beach-boys, why-don't-we-step-out-back, race-you-around-the-block guts to play a municipal golf course.

Down the No. 1 fairway at shortly after 6 a.m., as the sun pulls away from the horizon, displaying the hole in pink glow, there is still some fog, but you can see 14 guys trying to tee off. There is an official "starter," a retired gentleman with a microphone, who says, mostly during backswings, "Mr. Snodgrass next on the tee." If you venture forth alone you are paired with other jokers who generally range in handicap from four to 30. I got a used truck salesman and his buddy who sold books, a 17 and an 18, and one of the oldest men I have ever seen upright. During a splendid round last year he shot 134, about his age.

Hello, glad to meetcha. Me, oh, I'm an 8 handicap or so. The old guy and I will play them for two bucks a side, lowball. The old guy can't hear for beans. YOU AND ME. PARTNERS. TWO BUCKS. DOLLARS.

The tee area is roped off, like a bullfight. Behind, the thumps of practice swings echo off the asphalt. My partner has four clubs. Can he use my putter? Sure. SURE.

Mulligans—hitting drives, machine-gun style, until one finds the fairway—are as common as elm trees. The theory of mulligans at a municipal course is that 11 mulligans are no worse than one. If you are going to violate the Rules of Golf you might as well go ahead and violate the heck out of them. Golf balls are flying from the tee. I promise you that for the briefest of moments, both our opponents were teeing off at the same time.

The law of averages once again prevailed and they are down the middle.

My partner nudges it dead left into the driving range, and he plays one with a stripe around it.

Once on the course you must adjust your game and your behavior. It is not uncommon to be "hit into," which can result in serious injury, not to mention bogey. On one municipal course I saw a man hit into a group, the drive coming within inches of a skull. The player owning the skull walked back to the tee and hit a perfect 9-iron across the forehead of the man owning the driver. The latter passed out, cold. Somebody called an ambulance. No big deal. Par for the course.

It is not unusual to find strange objects in municipal sand traps, even bones. Some players think the rake by the side of the trap is a hazard itself, and that it is a two-stroke penalty if you touch it. Putting out of a trap was invented on a municipal course. Also, throwing it out of a trap. Also, leaving it in a trap.

There are many reasons why play tends to be slow on a municipal golf course. A main one is that a golf ball, however wounded, is a sacred object, and when one is hit into wood, over road or into water, it is searched for. Other people's balls also are searched for. A view of the public course from above must look like the biggest Easter egg hunt of all time.

Another reason for slow play is inferior play. When you seven-putt a green, it takes time. When you forget where the green is, it takes time to find it. When you stop to climb a fence and get a Coke from an adjoining supermarket, it takes time.

You are always hearing, "Excuse my buddy here, he is just learning."

Another reason is that nobody lets you play through, as if it were a sin. You ask to play through, then put 'em up and get ready to fight. Hit into them, they will hit back, and pretty soon it will be just like volleyball. It is as if letting somebody play through means you are a sissy.

As we completed No. 9 at 10 a.m. there was much teaching activity on the practice tee. It takes a real man to give lessons at a municipal course. You must spot improvement in a series of flailing arms, you must iron out slices, fade hooks and keep a straight face because no, Mr. Whomple, it isn't like croquet.

A municipal golf course is two parts, the front nine and the back nine. It is not a whole. There were six groups on the ninth tee, one of which should have been there, five of which had sneaked on when the back nine attendant, age 16, ran off after a girl from the pool.

We waited a six-pack worth, 35 minutes. My partner napped. I read half of a 200-page novel, and our opponents went to practice putts on the 18th green, which was near. When I looked up there were nine golf balls on the green, and the group coming up the 18th fairway was only a sixsome. Illegal, but fun.

The 18th is appropriately uphill, and, as the most logical placement of all, the bar and grill is just behind. You could fly one there and remain. The grill is what it is all about, the place where competitors fret over the scorecard as if it were Form 1040, shoes off, bag lumped in a corner, beer frothing, body still rippling like you just drove Kansas City to Las Vegas, non-stop.

This is where you add the eights and nines and discover where the $4 is headed. The money is handled gently, like a Masters' jacket. Losers crumple the proof, scorecard, as if it had been a poorly selected ticket at the $2 window. The sandwiches are the greatest, the beer the coldest, the companionship the best.

Remember No. 17? Flew an 8-iron. Flew it over the green, over the water fountain, over the fence, over the road. Should have choked a wedge.

Sometimes you have to go as far back as No. 2 to find that one crisp shot that will bring you back. My partner is exhausted, pale. I get some beer in him and he wants to go nine more. We make a game for next week and we are good friends.

To hundreds of thousands who go to drive-in movies, shop sales, buy golf balls at the drug store and putt from 10 yards off the green this is the only game in town.

It is the same great game they play on television for all that bread. When you check to see who is watching the next big tournament it will be the same person who is out Saturday morning, elbowing his way onto the first tee, wearing a baseball cap and a dedicated look.

Golf is great because you can give it to the people. If you want to watch some of us play, I'll give you a ring some morning about 5, but if you want to come later and start on 13, well, who's to know. Right, Mac?

Just bring your lunch.

THE SEARCH FOR THE PERFECT SET OF STICKS

by PETER DOBEREINER

Breathes there a man with soul so dead, who never to himself has said: "If only my clubs were exactly right, I'd belt the ball right out of sight."

Sitting in my study I can count 140 golf clubs displayed around the room or stacked in a corner. Most of them are, to a greater or lesser degree, antiques. But more than 30 are modern and still in regular use. When the fancy takes me I can select, say, a splendid old rut-iron and hit a few shots with a bramble pattern guttie in the garden. Or I might compare the feel of a McEwan long spoon with a carbon-fiber shafted driver by whacking plastic balls.

None of this makes me an expert on golf equipment. But I defer to no man in my experience as a victim of the neglected golfing disease known as Waggle. Twitch, or Yips, is the fashionable golfing ailment. Waggle, let me tell you, is much more virulent and painfully expensive.

Wagglers, as sufferers from this complaint are known, are basically obsessed by the thought expressed in those lines of doggerel at the top of the page. They devote their lives to a search for the perfect golf clubs. They believe—and often enough they are quite right—that their present clubs are costing them several shots a round.

And so they mope around pro shops, waggling away at the display sets. When playing with strangers they suddenly remark: "Those clubs look nice; mind if I have a bash with one of them?" In extreme cases they resort to do-it-yourself experiments with their clubs, grinding the irons, altering the lofts, lengthening the shafts and goose-necking the hosels.

Whenever I look up, my eye catches a spoon fitted with a pistol grip, which seems to mock me. It is a silent witness to the folly of the waggler (who, in turn, can testify that this experiment, designed to cure an over-strong left-hand position, was an abject failure).

Waggle is incurable. But eventually the disease enters a stage when it can be contained. The victim finally comes to realize that his own shortcomings as a golfer are to blame for his scores, rather than deficiencies in his equipment. This climacteric can go either way. The waggler may fall into a deep melancholy and go quietly mad.

He then rationalizes his situation. What is a scratch golfer, anyway? He is doing no more than the riveter in a shipyard who smacks the rivet with his hammer right on the bounce every time. So what sort of a big deal is that? Furthermore, I enjoy my bad golf enormously while it is a matter of simple observation to conclude that the good players are desperately unhappy. The fact that neither of these assertions bears much relation to the truth is beside the point.

With the addictive phase safely past, the waggler is now free to develop his interest in clubs for its own sake. The other day I was playing with a 3-handicap golfer who was turning on some impressive stuff with his irons. I forbore to ask if I might try one of his clubs, since that stage is safely under control nowadays, but I was interested in the flighting of his shots and asked what shafts he had. To my amazement he had to inspect the label and then said: "R, whatever that means."

That man is content—but I feel, nevertheless, that he is missing quite a lot through his complete disinterest in the form and development of clubs. I would not wish him a dose of the waggles but there is a happy and rewarding medium.

In some ways golf must have been a much better game 200 years ago when the first clubs were being formed. With their peacock uniforms and gargantuan club suppers from which no member retired with less than a gallon of claret in his belly, the golfers of Edinburgh were indeed favored. Their actual golf, I imagine, was not up to much. Their clubs were all woods, of course, at that time, carried higgledy-piggledy under the arm of a ruffianly (and frequently drunk) caddie.

And the ball they played was what we refer to as the featherie, although many were stuffed with hemp, flax or straw. By all accounts the featherie could be a very good ball but it was a lottery whether you got a round one. In wet weather it soon lost what shape it had. As for the techniques of golf, we know from the inordinate length of those clubs that you had to swing very flat with a pronounced sway at the knees.

I don't suppose they minded much. After all, in their terms, the equipment was a vast improvement on the even longer and heavier clubs and boxwood balls, which had been the golfer's lot for 200 years.

In the earliest days the making of clubs and balls was the domain of bow-makers. These craftsmen had a long tradition in working with beech and split-ash shafts and they naturally turned to these woods for making the implements for this frivolous sport.

But waggle virus was in the air and men dreamed of having

such clubs as would transform them into the finest players the world had known. On reflection, perhaps the middle of the 19th century was the golden age of golf. It was at this time that the game made a significant advance. The guttie ball was introduced and at once the wooden clubs had to undergo changes to accommodate the unyielding impact of the new ball. Beech was too hard for the guttie and the new generation of clubmakers turned to woods like apple and pear.

Some golfers tried to modify their clubs by facing them with patches of leather to soften the shock of impact but this was merely a temporary palliative.

Men like Hugh Philp, whose skill as a clubmaker was never surpassed, fashioned beautiful clubs which are recognized today as works of art. A gentleman golfer would go to Philp (or to Douglas McEwan, James Wilson or Robert Forgan) in the same spirit as he might visit his tailor, to be "fitted."

We can imagine Philp selecting blackthorn heads (specially planted on a bank so that the stem would bend naturally to make the "scare") and then the two of them discussing which were the pick of the latest consignment of hickory shafts.

Everyone specified Tennessee hickory but the real cognoscenti insisted on shafts from the central strip of Tennessee. Lowland hickory was too soft; that from the high ground was brittle.

Philp would then get to work with saw, spoke-shave, plane, rasp, file and chisel to fashion the heads and then gouge them out into delicate shells to be filled with lead. With the heads spliced to the shafts and finished with a hare's foot dipped in a mixture of oil and varnish, the customer would return to waggle and pronounce verdict.

Perhaps this one's a fraction stiffer than the others. "Certainly, sir." Philp would then shave a micromillimeter off the shaft, or pretend to, and the customer would depart with a set of clubs which were—and I choose my words with due deliberation— better matched than anything you can buy today.

What is more, and here I voice a purely personal opinion, the grips of untanned hide over a layer of felt-like cloth were better than anything available today.

Apart from the need for a more robust form of head, and a softer one, in the woods, the guttie stimulated development of iron-headed clubs. The iron, previously used mainly as a specialist club for recovering from cart tracks, followed a similar process of sophistication, with a few lunatic aberrations along the way.

They were an inventive race, those clubmakers, and whenever I read modern advertisements with all their pseudo-scientific mumbo-jumbo about reducing the weight of the hosel and putting it where it counts, I take down a number of early irons which have had holes bored in the hosel for that very purpose. There really is very little that is new in golf clubs. Somewhere, sometime, somebody has tried it before—and that goes for speed slots and aerodynamic-shaped heads and all the modern gobbledy-gook, not excluding heel-and-toe balance.

On even further reflection, there is much to be said for golf in the 20th century. The boy who learned his golf with the guttie was a good, accurate striker—because he had to be. Anything of a mis-hit sent a shock through the fingers like 5,000 volts, but shortly after the turn of the century the rubber-core ball became available.

Now, surely, was the day of the waggler. Although I have cited an imaginary example of a man ordering a full set from Hugh Philp, the more common practice was to acquire clubs one by one. You would waggle club after club until that magic moment when you knew that this was the niblick for you. How long that love affair lasted depended on you and the niblick, but meanwhile the search went on for the perfect mashie.

Yes, for sheer golfing pleasure those must have been the days and there are happily still many golfers among us who can confirm that judgment. Imagine a beautiful spring morning in the 20's, with income tax at sixpence in the pound, God in his heaven and Britannia ruling the waves.

You pull into Sunningdale gaily humming the Charleston, narrowly missing the Prince of Wales on his way out, and dive into Jack White's shop. There you find a new driver, perfect in every detail, and thus complete a set of absolutely true loves. You tee up a brand new rubber-core and let fly.

There are two attractions about hitting the golf ball: the effect on you and the effect on the ball itself. I believe that in the combination of a good hickory-shafted club and a rubber-core ball these twin satisfactions reached their happiest compromise. You may get more distance with a steel or carbon-fiber shafted club, but you lose on the sensuous feel which hickory produces when you catch her square on the button.

Of all the clubs I have ever swung or waggled, nothing reproduces that feel which I get from a driver with a scored shaft stamped with the name of Harry Vardon which I have in my collection. They don't make clubs like that anymore.

All that disappeared with the 30's and the coming of steel, and no amount of nostalgia can disguise the fact that progress brought with it many advantages for the golfer. Some dreadful clubs were produced in the early days of steel. You can still find some real clinkers in the latest models but, generally speaking, golf clubs have a high standard today. Many people say there were clubs 20 years ago every bit as good as today's, and they may be right. I think it is true to say that you had to be lucky, or very astute, to get a good set in the 50's whereas today you have to be unlucky or stupid to get a bad set.

One of the symptoms of the waggler in the post-addictive stage is that he becomes cautious to the point of cynicism. There

96

was a time when the mere mention of the expression "Spoiler stabilizer" (yes, it is true. Fitted on woods, like grand prix cars) would have me negotiating a second mortgage in order to get one. "Keeps the club closer to the ground and provides more stability as the clubhead zips through the hitting area." Of course! That's the answer! I must have one. Nowadays I react to that sort of claim with a short and extremely vulgar expletive and turn the page.

The difficulty arises from the fact that the same advertising copywriters are employed to laud the virtues of the worthless gimmicks and the genuine advances in design. How can we consumers detect the difference? You won't go far wrong if you ignore any claim involving a fancy name, like "Speed groove" and if, in addition, it involves a bastardized spelling such as "Pinseeka" you can be fairly certain that it's not for you.

On the development of golf balls, my guess is that the trend will be to tougher balls, with a hybrid between the rubber-core and the indestructible solid coming along shortly.

If you tell me that I am hopelessly naive to imagine that manufacturers will produce an uncuttable top-quality ball, and so kill their own market, then I admit the possibility. But I live in hopes with my childish belief in the goodness of human nature. Besides, the first manufacturer to produce such a ball will make a fortune and do his rivals down at the same time. That's human nature, too.

GOLF'S MENAGERIE

by JOSEPH C. DEY

Nature is awake. Squiggly things poke cold little noses out from under leaves and rocks. Larvae are about to become insects and grubs which soon will feast on tender, expensive turfgrass. Poa annua's deceitful flower is whitening. Yes, spring is bustin' out all over, and the golf course superintendent braces for the worst.

From other winterings emerge other foes of the course: big, two-legged foes who, unthinkingly, will now do their best—which means their worst—to undo the good work of nature and the superintendent. There are some at every club. They have never become golf-course-broken, though they may have played for years. Heedlessly, they will bash their way about with rarely a thought for the messy trail they leave and the expense they cost the club. They remind one of that indelicate sign in an old-time rural barber shop: "If you spit on the floor at home, do it here. We want you to feel at home."

Here are some of golf's human enemies—do you recognize them?

The Tee-Ripping Hyena: On every teeing ground he compulsively takes heavy-handed practice swings that tear turf, which takes weeks to grow and which he never repairs.

The Bunker Buffalo: Pawing and pawing until he stands knee-deep in the sand, he then explodes a half-ton of sand before the ball mercifully emerges. Then he climbs straight up the bunker face to the putting green, with never a care for cleaning up his mess and smoothing things for those who follow. (On the PGA tour, if he didn't make sure the bunker was put back in shape he'd be fined $150.)

The Divot-Killing Warthog: His fairway excavations put an archeologist to shame. Having flung a divot thither, he lets it lie and die, roots exposed to drying sun and wind; the hole he made becomes a permanent depression. If only he'd replace his divot, he'd help not only the turf but players coming after him, for there'd be no loose impediment for a ball to rest against nor a hole for a ball to lie in. Of course, some divots disintegrate so thoroughly they

98

would never take root again (as with some Bermuda grasses), but at least their holes can be partly filled and leveled. Although some Warthogs half heartedly replace divots, they do it imperfectly, leaving edges sticking out or upward; they thereby create rules problems, for cut turf replaced in position may not be removed or pressed down if the ball's lie would be affected.

The Rough-Riding Yak: Treats golf as another form of drag racing. Speeds all over in his car. Always selects the juiciest turf nearest the green to park his vehicle. Can't read; signs directing car traffic are wasted on him.

The Litterbug-Ostrich: A strange hybrid. The Litterbug in him leaves a trail of ball cartons, candy wrappers, torn-up scorecards. The Ostrich in him never sees them. Highly unpopular with greenkeeping staff.

The putting green is a favorite playground for several two-legged foes of a well-conditioned course. Consider these:

The Pitch-Mark Blind Pig: He never seems to see the little crater-and-mound combinations pushed up by his shots to the green, especially when the greens are soft. It would take him only a moment to repair one, like this: raise the area just outside the damage with a sharp-pointed object such as a green repair tool or a tee, lifting it toward the center of the damaged area, spreading any bunched-up turf, then flattening it. The rules allow stepping on such a place. But no—the Pitch-Mark Blind Pig leaves his trademark. If no good samaritan comes along to minister to it, the little mound of healthy putting-green turf is apt to be shorn off by a green mower at dawn's early light. (Some clubs have successfully campaigned for players to "Fix Yours and One More.")

The Foot-Dragging Slob: To watch him walk, you'd think he wore 50-pound shoes, so slovenly does he drag them. His trademark is unmistakable—jagged lines of turf torn by his spikes.

The Body-English Slue-Footed Yak: From childhood he has cherished a fantasy that, after striking a putt, he can direct the ball into the hole by twisting about in bodily contortions, feet first. A first cousin to the Foot-Dragging Slob.

The Rock-and-Roll Wildebeest (or Gnu): Highly emotional. On every putt, leaps in the air and comes down in either glee or disgust—his hoofmarks are the same in both cases.

The Flagstick-Flinging, Cup-Banging Baboon: A two-letter man. First, on yanking the flagstick from the hole, he tosses it on the green, thereby creating a bumpy little groove in the turf. Second, instead of replacing the flagstick tenderly, he throws it javelin-like into the hole, denting the side of the cup, which thereafter is never 4¼ inches in diameter and thus is "illegal."

For all their seeming differences, these members of golf's untamed menagerie have a common failing—they do not think of consequences. In their mindlessness, they inflict untold annoyances on fellow players, and they increase the cost of course maintenance appallingly. For them to say they are willing to pay the price is no answer at all. Money penalties cannot atone for bad manners.

A distinction of golf is its good manners—little courtesies which are part of the lubrication of living.

Before World War II the Etiquette of Golf was printed at the end of the Rules of Golf booklet. I well remember a thoughtful USGA chairman saying that the etiquette section should appear at the beginning of the code. So it was done, and so it is today.

"Bentley was in . . . played rather poorly."

"Young man . . . if I employ your inside swing,
I might very well beat myself to death."

"Here. Take what you'll need and I'll run
the car around back of the green."

GOLF IN DISNEYLAND

by JIM MURRAY

Golf in and around Los Angeles tends to be—like the rest of the landscape—unreal . . . part Royal & Ancient, part Disneyland. The Good Ship Lollipop with 4-irons. You expect a director to come walking out of the woods on 18 in puttees and with his cap on backward yelling, "Cut!"

The stuffy types at Blind Brook or Old Elm or The Country Club would never understand. There's a gaudy impermanence to Golf Hollywood that would shake the walrus mustaches right off the portraits in those staid old clubs. Remember, we're talking about an area where a chain-saw manufacturer bought the London Bridge and had it shipped over to provide a crossing over desert sand. They bought the Queen Mary and turned it into a chop house. They could buy St. Andrews and stick it up at La Quinta.

You get a running start toward understanding palm-tree, water pipe golf if you listen to that old joke about the sport in Los Angeles. Seems a man named Frank Rosenberg, a Texas oil man, wanted to get into Los Angeles Country Club, the West Coast version of the stodgiest and most exclusive club in the world. It is said eligibility for membership is a Hoover button, a home in Pasadena and proof-positive you never had an actor in the family. Once, when a member proposed Jimmy Roosevelt for membership, they not only blackballed the Roosevelt, they kicked out the member.

Rosenberg was rejected out of hand and the membership committeeman politely suggested he try Hillcrest. Hillcrest is a golf course which was founded by a movie man who was snubbed at a Pasadena course because of his religion. It has fewer gentiles than a kibbutz.

Rosenberg was stunned to be rejected by L.A.C.C. and he so confided to a friend. "Oh," suggested the friend, "they probably thought you were Jewish. The club is restricted."

So Rosenberg applied at Hillcrest. "Fine, we'll take your application and wait for the first opening," he was told. "Fine," said Rosenberg, "but there's one other thing I want you to know—

102

I'm not Jewish."

The committeeman looked at him and said softly, "Oh, dear. I'm sorry. We don't admit gentiles." "Well, I'm an s.o.b.!" exploded Rosenberg. "If you can prove that," the committeeman told him, "you can get into Riviera!"

Riviera may be the most beautiful of the L.A. area courses. But it's a monster. It is the only southern California golf course ever to host the Open. Hogan won it there in 1948. It's a demanding 7,100-yard, par-71 track no weekend player should be abroad on. Its rolls list mostly ruthless golfers, not card-players, not social members, but guys who can shoot in the 70's anywhere in the world.

It used to be a hustler's paradise. The stories are legendary (also libelous) of the dentists, Filipino generals, European counts, carefree movie stars and moguls who got fleeced on its not-so-broad fairways. It was Titanic Thompson country. You could get a bet on the color of the next dog coming up the fairway. It is Dean Martin's happy hunting ground as this is written and Dino is usually marauding on its tees and eucalyptus trees in division strength. It looks like Hitler's armor coming down the back side. Martin usually has three or four foursomes (or fivesomes) of pals, usually including one name pro (Devlin, Floyd, Bayer or Bolt), and the bets flow two or three holes back. Barry Jaeckel, French Open winner and son of a movie star, used to caddie for Dino, who has a reputation for having lost a fortune at the game. If so, he did it some time ago. Dean now is recognized around Riviera as a guy you give strokes to at your own peril. All the same, the trading is livelier among those golf cars than it is on the Paris Bourse. I know a lot of people who would like to cut 10 percent of it and retire to the French Riviera after one season.

So, if golf is your bag, get into Riviera. They don't care what your religion or background is there. But they hope you have money and are willing to risk it. Mac Hunter, the pro there, was once considered a better prospect than Arnold Palmer and may hold the record for a club pro making cuts in the U.S. Open. His dad won the British Amateur and his son won the California Amateur at Pebble Beach. If a guy says he's from Riviera, be sure to say, "We'll adjust at the turn," or you may go home in a barrel.

L.A. Country Club, apart from its exclusivity, is noteworthy because it sits athwart what must be the most expensive cluster of real estate in the world. It is almost in the center of Beverly Hills and its two golf courses have nearly a mile of front footage along Wilshire Boulevard. It is a 2-iron from Saks Fifth Avenue, I. Magnin, Tiffany's and the most expensive furriers and jewelers and boutiques in the world. The Beverly Hilton Hotel hangs over it. Imagine a golf course on either side of Fifth Avenue from 38th Street to the 80's and extending for 250 acres in all directions, and you have a notion of the Big Rock Candy Mountain that is L.A.C.C. Some countries couldn't afford to buy it.

You can get into L.A. Country Club for about $25,000, but, since you get a piece of the action, that's not as steep as it sounds. With 800 members, this computes out at $2 million for the property. I'd like to get it at that price.

Country clubs are social dinosaurs. Their mores, rules and lifestyles are right out of the 19th century and they might have become as extinct as the saber-toothed tiger were it not for the ecological uproar. Now they are popularly regarded, even by the fiercest of environmental militants, as "green belts." Even though they are refuges for those other dinosaurs, the entrenched millionaires, they are grudgingly tolerated, even by the anarchists.

But most of the clubs in L.A. suddenly canvassed their rolls and found they read like a headstone count in a cemetery. Something like 20 percent of the memberships in one country club were owned by estates, part of the last will and testament of J. Rotten Rich, who has long since gone to that Great-Fairway-In-The-Sky. Ghosts don't buy drinks or alpacas or patronize the Thursday night dance, and the rigor mortis eventually would hit the club, too. Accordingly, the clubs took to offering $5,000 non-equity memberships to qualified applicants UNDER 40, the fee payable in two installments. All three of the high-priced L.A. clubs, Bel-Air ($13,500 plus $85 a month dues), Lakeside ($11,500 plus $75 dues) and L.A. ($100 a month after the initiation) offer the "youth" memberships.

If Riviera is the club for golfers and L.A. the club for oil, orange and railroad barons, Bel-Air attracts the management end of the broadcast and movie media. There are more station managers, network West Coast brass and their satellite advertising agency account executives (with a sprinkling of used-car dealers) at Bel-Air than at any other club in America.

It once was a club for L.A. Country Club rejects. It, too, sits astride some of the world's richest real estate, and it used to be a sandbox for the movie rich. Bing Crosby once belonged here. Fred MacMurray, Ray Bolger, Andy Williams play here and the Show-Biz types, the talent, shower downstairs. The upstairs locker room is, fittingly, the executive suite. The talent handlers—directors, agents, press agents, producers, ad men and network veepees shower up here.

Dean Martin was a daily communicant at Bel-Air until a green committeeman cut up the greens to "improve" the course, a venture that was to prove long and, therefore, costly, because Dino and dozens of others quit in protest at having to play temporary greens. The departure of a Dean Martin from a golf club is comparable to a nearsighted millionaire leaving a crap game in a smoky room.

Lakeside has a charisma all its own. Here, in the salad years, the movie greats gamboled . . . Laurel and Hardy, W. C. Fields, Crosby, Hope, Jack Carson, Dennis Morgan, Gordon MacRae and

Johnny Weissmueller drank here. Across the street from Warner Bros., it was a happy hunting ground for Warner's stars, who were not of the same magnitude as MGM's in those years but were a whole lot more festive. A requirement at Lakeside was that you be able to hold your booze. That was the club of the hard-drinking Irish and, the gag, a standard for admission, was that you had to be able to kill a fifth in nine holes.

Disc jockeys, industrial press agents, radio announcers (radio!) still dot Lakeside's membership rolls. The Old Guard is almost all gone (Buddy Rogers and Richard Arlen still play, for you trivia buffs). Only Bob Hope remains and fits in a fast nine holes on the infrequent occasions he is at home. Crosby kept a locker but hadn't used it in years. The hard core of Lakeside is made up of guys who made it in the Big Band Era. It's THE club to belong to if you live in the lace-curtain sections of the Valley. Like Bel-Air, it has a slightly more modern step to it, as reflected in its club-house and dining areas. It's a golf course for the well-heeled stubborn types. Unlike the muttonchop-sideburns courses like L.A., it has no trouble making the bar and restaurant pay off, but like them, its club flag is at half-mast too often these days.

Wilshire Country Club is almost in downtown L.A. This makes it accessible to judges, lawyers, business executives, railroad and bank presidents. Color it dull gray.

The city's most celebrated golfers long were Hope and Crosby. Crosby in his prime was a solid 2, but he drifted away from the grand old game in favor of bird-shooting and game-fishing. But not before he whooshed a few practice shots off the 10th tee at Bel-Air one afternoon (Bel-Air has no practice range) and a member of the green committee came out and stuffily ordered Der Bingle to cease and desist. Crosby looked at him with that cold look a friend once described as "Arctic blue," the look that could stave in the bow of the Titanic. And Crosby gravely packed his clubs, emptied his locker—and was not seen at Bel-Air again. W. C. Fields was fond of playing the course sideways with his pal, Oliver Hardy. He liked being in the trees where he could drink without scandalizing the natives.

Mickey Rooney holds the unique distinction of being thrown out of Lakeside. The Mick was a solid 3 in his best days, but he was not only a club-thrower, he threw whole sets. He once played the front nine with a new set and, at the turn, junked them and bought another new one for the back nine.

Playing with Mickey is like playing in the middle of a rehearsal for a Broadway musical. Mickey will sing the score, act the parts. He will do Judy Garland and Professor Labermacher (an old Jessel routine). He showed up on the first tee one day proudly announcing that Jack Nicklaus, no less, had straightened out his swing. As he moved flawlessly through the first three holes, he purred with praise for the new set of stiff shafts he had purchased. He

105

dispensed tips with a lavish hand for the rest of the foursome. By hole 5, the swing began to disintegrate. By hole 9, the Mick was looking darkly at his new set of clubs and beginning to question Nicklaus' credentials to be teaching golf. By the back side, Mickey was holding the clubs aloft to anyone who would listen and demanding, "I ask you! Just look at these things! Look at the hosel! How can a man play with implements like these!" If you're a Mickey Rooney fan, you're rolling behind the trees, helpless with mirth. Mickey's funnier when he's not trying to be. But the members got tired of ducking in the showers when Mickey came through looking for a game, and they told him to empty his locker.

At Hillcrest, the game is "Can-You-Top-This?" and I don't mean a golf ball. There is a table at Hillcrest that is a shrine of Show Business. George Burns, Jack Benny, George Jessel, Eddie Cantor and Al Jolson used to lunch in a shower of one-liners. Every noon was a Friar's Roast. Danny Thomas represents the Catholics at Hillcrest. In the days of the Dusenberg-Bugatti-leopard-on-a-leash Hollywood, more picture deals were set here than at neighboring Twentieth Century-Fox, which is just across the street and is gradually giving way to a high-rise subdivision. The opulence of Hillcrest is Hapsburgian. The chandeliered dining room makes the Queen Mary foyer look like a lunch counter. The Marx brothers (save for Groucho, who disapproved of golf courses because there weren't enough girls) were the best players in the comedians' flight.

Brentwood, referred to as "Hillcrest East," plays host to the newest crop of comedians—Joey Bishop, Don Rickles, Don Adams (who also belongs at Riviera) and the generation of stand-up comics who came along in the television-Las Vegas era. Brentwood is not as severe a test of golf as L.A.C.C.'s North Course or Hillcrest, but successive renovations have given its clubhouse more and more of a Taj Mahal look.

Brentwood is important historically, because it was to have been the site of the 1962 PGA. The California attorney general threatened legal action because of the PGA's "Caucasian only" clause, and the PGA in 1961 jerked the tournament to friendlier climes at Aronomink in Philadelphia. But later in '61 the offending phrase was removed from the by-laws and the way was paved on tour for the Charlie Siffords, Lee Elders and George Johnsons.

Los Angeles probably has more "celebrity" tournaments per square foot than any golfing area in the world. Any golfing actor worth his marquee value would rather be caught without his makeup on camera than without a favorite charity. As Jerry Lewis once complained, "By the time I arrived, all the diseases were taken." George Jessel once observed that all that was left for the newcomers was gonorrhea. Chuck Connors has a tournament. A Tim Conway, a Bob Stack and even character actors have tournaments of their own. Even the tour fixtures have reached out to embrace celebrities. The celebrities trade guest appearances at each other's tournaments, and the star power attracts the Kansas City wheat merchants to pay out a grand to tee it up with some crooner or TV tough guy in the pro-am.

Humphrey Bogart, it may surprise you to know, was very nearly a scratch golfer. Once a journalist drinking buddy of his put this reputation down to side-of-the-mouth braggadocio. Bogey, who rarely made one, took his pal down to Tamarisk and proceeded to rip off an impeccable 73 after not playing for two months.

It's a game for all seasons in California. You can play golf 365 days a year. Every private club is awash with entertainment giants and sports greats. You might bump into a Jerry West (but not in the rough) at Riviera or a Jim Brown at Western Avenue (a flat muni-type club where the membership is largely black). The Dodgers' Don Sutton will be at Oakmont in the off-season, as will half the franchise. The Rams are addicts.

It's not a game uniquely suited to a community famed for its happy endings. John Wayne ducked the game throughout his career, even though his whole stock company, including Grant Withers and Ward Bond and Forrest Tucker, was scattered around Lakeside, where Wayne had a membership. The official reason was that "a golf ball just isn't Duke's size." The screenwriter, James Edward Grant, had a better explanation: "How could a guy who won the West, recaptured Bataan and won the battle of Iwo Jima let himself be defeated by a little hole in the ground?"

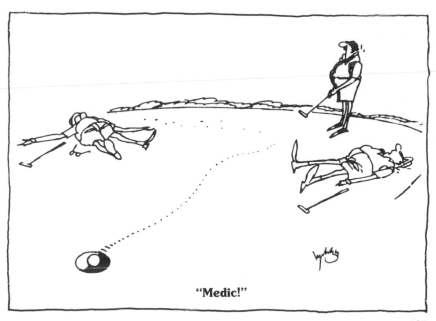

"Medic!"

THE PERILS OF THE GAME

by HENRY LONGHURST

There seems little doubt that the humble, pedestrian game of golf is getting more dangerous every day, partly through the inability of the thousands of newcomers to the game (and, come to that, the old stagers, too) to hit the ball even remotely in the direction they are aiming and partly because the game induces such violent passions as to cause golfers to set upon each other with clubs, sticks and any other weapons that come to hand.

I would give much, for instance, to have had a ringside seat at the Battle of Silver Spring, Md., when a four-ball complained that the players just in front were particularly slow, and decided to "play through 'em." This they attempted to do, with the result that the first of their drives was dispatched by the people in front deliberately into the woods.

When the two groups met, a free-for-all broke out, resulting in three bent clubs, one broken club, one wound requiring seven stitches, several other head wounds and one fractured skull. The information that reached my side of the Atlantic was that a county grand jury had indicted one of the offenders on three charges of assault, including one with intent to murder.

Many of the more senior golfers will remember the tall, craggy figure of Archie Compston, professional at the Mid-Ocean Club, Bermuda. His teaching methods were forceful and direct and not every pupil could "take" them. One who decided to stand up to him was the beautiful Virginia, the Marchioness of Northampton, who became so incensed that she hit him vigorously on the shin. I asked her what club she took. An 8-iron. And what did he do? "He bellowed," she said. A pretty little scene.

Few games have furnished lawyers with such a profitable amount of litigation as golf—nor, on the whole, such profitless litigation for the golfers. As courses proliferate, often on flat terrain with less and less ground between parallel holes, a sliced drive which in earlier days would probably have been lost in the woods is now likely to bean some luckless fellow on an adjacent fairway. The injured party, however, tends to get little sympathy from the courts if he sues. This seems to apply equally in the United States and Britain.

In London, for instance, some years ago a player hooked his drive from the 11th tee and struck another member on the 16th, smashing his glasses and causing him to lose the sight of one eye. The case, such is the speed of British justice, came up three years later and the man who lost his eye was awarded nothing.

"The case turned eventually on the question of negligence," one of the lawyers concerned told me, "and it was held that a golfer could not be considered negligent merely because he did not hit the ball along the line on which he had been aiming."

This, and similarly hard-hearted decisions in American courts, gave rise to much discussion and uncertainty on golfers' insurance policies. What, it was held, was the use of insuring against damage to your person if you had to prove negligence—and a man who takes your eye out from an adjacent fairway is not held to be negligent?

On the other hand, a lady from St. Louis, whose drive struck another lady who was obscured by a tree at the time, was held by a Missouri court to have been negligent and ordered to pay $5,000 in damages.

Another who lost an eye, at Deauville, France, in 1919, was Mr. Jimmy de Rothschild, who was wearing a monocle, which he continued to wear for the rest of his life. A great art connoisseur and racehorse owner and for many years a Member of Parliament, this popular figure lived for another 40 years and left £11 million. He did not need to sue anyone.

On the other hand, a 15-year-old caddie at a club in Galesburg, Ill., just before World War II was stung by a bee on the course and as a result became blind. He sued the club and was awarded the maximum damages. Good for the boy, but it seems a little harsh if a club is to be held responsible for the actions of its bees.

The perils of golf are an ongoing part of the game. The Cambridge University golf club in England has just celebrated its centenary. One of its founders was W. T. Linskill, and the other day I came across a little booklet he wrote at the turn of the century. "It is ridiculous," he says, "to suggest, as some people do, that golf is a dangerous game. I myself have only been struck three times this season!"

"Kind of excited about that birdie, eh, Fred?"

"OK if my brother comes along for the laughs?"

"Does dew really bother you that much?"

"And when he's not on the course he's pacing off imaginary
yardage on imaginary shots for imaginary holes."

ARM-WRESTLING
THE BLUE MONSTER

by WILLIAM PRICE FOX

Miami International Airport. Rented a car and copied directions carefully for Doral Country Club. Headed out into the night and made wrong turn. Made another. Dead end. Lost. People shorter, darker, rattling off machine-gun Spanish. Signs in windows: "English spoken here." Would hope so. Asked directions. Gave Doral the Spanish pronunciation. Cuban in thonged sandals gave me roads and mileages. Also English lesson. Doral not Spanish. Combination of Doris and Al Kaskel. Offered me a dark cigarette. "Be sure and play the Blue Monster."

Headed out 34th Street. Bell-hopped on Beach here in 50's. Big tax-free money days. Straight tips, no salary. Used to know the city, but not anymore. Shopping malls and high-risers now where the armadillo and iguana used to roam. Real-estate sharks filled in swamps. Sold it fast before it sunk. Trees still the same. Royal palms, coconut palms, palmettos. Up in pink-lighted live oak, mocking birds singing everything but theme song from Zhivago.

Spanish music on radio. Trumpets and wild flamenco guitars. Since fifties 400,000 Cubans have moved in. Improved the music and the night life. Clubs open until three. Package stores until midnight. Restaurants serve breakfast 24 hours a day. Doral sign is green on flat white. Guard at gate. Swing around circle into main entrance. Doral beautiful, also big—660 rooms. Four courses: Red, White, Blue, Gold.

Fruit and cheese basket in room with complimentary bottle of German wine. Complete with corkscrew for wine, knife for cheese. Management's idea for return business. Smart. Investment too steep for today's bellhop. Minimum wage law has destroyed the fire and creativity. Used to be a great profession. Bellhop showed me where light switch, john and a/c controls were. No imagination as in old days. Should have tried for car wash, dry cleaning, laundry, booze, sandwich, ladies of the night. Bellhops today too lazy to work, too nervous to steal. Could have given him sage advice, but too late for him. Either have it naturally or don't. Tipped him $5 for old days. Should have given him $2.

112

Slept like stone. Up early. Breakfast in coffee shop and on to see golf director Tony Turiano. Told him I had a 12 but wasn't playing to it. Sympathetic. Understanding. Said it happens all the time. Had another 12-handicapper who wasn't playing to his, either. Suggested we play shorter Red Course first. Billed as executive course. Unlike executive steaks, which come bigger, thicker and more expensive, executive courses are shorter, wider. Little or no rough. Makes sense. Teamed me with Leonard Murphy, Garden City, Long Island, New York.

Leonard OK. Tall, thin. Articulated spider swing. At last split second a miracle of corrections, and ball comes off clubface hot. Unfortunately, it hooks. We both hook. Close together on every shot. Doral requires cars on all courses at all times. Speeds up play. In season 1,000 golfers a day. All want 9 a.m. "Blue Monster" tee-off time. Tony Turiano spreads them out and keeps them happy.

Conveyor belt brings clubs from storage to car area. Everything streamlined to give maximum golf for money. Foursome leaves tee every seven or eight minutes. Everything works, no slippage. Each tee equipped with painting of hole showing water, sand, green shape and out-of-bounds. Tees flat, manicured like greens. Greens perfect. Fairways cut short for good lies and you can come down hard on all shots. Might be a factory, but a good one.

With identical hooks we finish Red with identical scores of 83. Not bad for first day. Leonard had been on phone with girlfriend at pool. "She's never tired. I come in from 36 holes, I want to eat and watch Kojak and go to sleep. She wants to go nightclubbing. Mistake coming down here with her. Too much to do."

Leonard is right, what with dog tracks, horse racing, jai alai, scuba diving, deep-sea fishing and half of Hollywood out on the Beach in the big clubs.

"Hell, I came down for the golf. Well, at least she's getting a tan."

Play Red Course again, getting ready for "Blue Monster" and the Gold. Win by four. Should have been 10, but couldn't putt. Decide to practice. Bronze bust of Al Kaskel overlooking putting green. A bust has to overlook something. Would do better smiling out over the 18th on the Blue.

Doral very successful. PGA tour event played here every year. Nicklaus wins his share. This year it was Andy Bean. The big lug threw his ball to the gallery after holing out on 18, the way the champs do, and hurt his shoulder. Every hacker wants to arm-wrestle the "Blue Monster." One low, squat merchant from Detroit explained how he played it.

"OK. I hit a nice tee shot. Down the middle 170-175. I hit another not so nice. But see, I still ain't in the water. Then I push one. A wood. Now I'm getting closer and I'm still not in trouble. OK, I'm on. Almost." He opens his hands smiling. "I'm settling for a nice 8."

Tell Leonard about the Cuban and how Doral means Doris and Al. He tells me that New York Biltmore was named for Vander-BILT and MORgan. Leonard a practical man who has seen sins of the times. Composed dissatisfaction, but tolerant of everything.

"The Beach is dying. Everything's moving up to Lauderdale and Boca Raton." Pointed his putter at the bust of Al Kaskel. "Al here was smart. Put his money in golf. He stuck it out. The rest of them out on the Beach are starving. I been coming here two, three times a year for 15 years now. The Beach they can have. Retirees. That's all they've got out there. You go into the Fountain-bleu in the summertime and what do you see? Hippies, Hare Krishnas, Moonies all running around barefoot and selling peanut brittle. I tell you it breaks my heart seeing that."

Leonard a geo-politician and social scientist. Makes his living in potato chip and pretzel business. "When the college girls started going to Lauderdale, that's when it all began to fall apart. People follow the girls. OK, they like the rooms, the beach, the horses. They like the nightlife. But guys like me and you are always looking. Always. Never can tell when something nice is going to break your door down. They haven't built a new hotel here in 15 years. Lauderdale, that's where they're building." He rubbed Al's bronzed head. "How about it, Al? Ain't that right?"

Play Leonard the second day. Blue Course, 7,000 yards, par 72. Third, fourth, eighth, ninth, 10th and 18th holes over water. From low-flying plane, Blue and Gold courses look more like waterskiing marina than golf course. Fear of water and four-inch-high Bermuda grass rough takes its toll. Heavy Florida air, lush fairways with little roll conspire to keep score up. More trouble with water on left than playing over it. Hooked four balls in for a 91. Leonard three balls for 86.

Leonard complaining he wasn't getting enough sleep to make a full turn. Girlfriend didn't want to come in until 3 a.m. Wanted to dance. Drink Mai Tais. Wanted to talk. Wanted him. Slept from 5 till 8. "I can't do it on three hours anymore. These par 4's are killing me." Par 4's all over 410.

Strolled around the lobby. Doral one of best convention centers in the country. Hall of the Conquerors leads into huge Conquistador Room. Big meeting and dining hall. Murals depicting the triumphs of Magellan, Cortez, Balboa. Ponce de Leon looking as if he found the fountain here at Doral and had the franchise for selling the waters.

On last day I had choice of Blue or Gold, and took the Gold. Leonard in bed. Too tired. So I played alone. First hole 523 yards, par 5. First tee shot hooked deep into rough. Hit "Mulligan." Hooked again. Third tee shot straight. Played third shot. Lying one. Played second ball off second shot and third ball off third. Told myself I was warming up. Knew I was lying. On green 40 feet from cup. Hit three series of putts. Finally down in two. No one three-putts when alone. Put down 5 on card. Some guilt, but not much. Course clear in front. Course clear in back. X'd out 5. Decided to turn over new leaf and play an honest game. Renew respect in self.

Did 180-degree turn. Returned to first tee. Tony didn't see me. This time one ball and one ball only. No gimmes, no improved lies. Score would be my real score. Real score which I would carry through life. Maybe tattoo on arm. The Gold Course would tell me the truth.

Off to good start. Parred first with two putts. Hook easing up. Playing one ball philosophically sound. Have spent nights on driving range pounding out five and six buckets. Faster and faster. Nothing counted so nothing mattered. But Gold round at Doral mattered. Yes. Parred second. On ninth I was two over par. Getting nervous, giddy.

Called Leonard from halfway house. Girlfriend: "He's busy. Can he call you?" Could tell they'd been arguing.

I needed a witness. Then decided I didn't, could trust myself. Never did before, but this time different. Brand-new start. Would use same lucky Titleist, 90 compression, No. 7. Would touch ball only on greens. Then only to clean off mud. Strictest USGA summer rules. A birdie on 10, then four straight pars. On 15th tough decision who to play in with. Dave Marr at Cypress Point? Trevino at St. Andrews? Would be in 70's. Could play with anyone. Nicklaus? Why not? Practice round at Masters. No crowd. Just the two of us, so we could talk.

Tied 15th with him. He rolled in 60-footer for bird on 16. Caught him on 17th. My honors on 18. Drove longest ball down center. He was having trouble pulling ball. Gave him tip on right elbow flying. He tried it and hit it flush. Thanked me, saying he couldn't believe it was that simple. His ball long but 10 yards short of mine.

"Listen Jack. You've got friends watching from the clubhouse. Hit my ball. It'll look better. I'm really an unknown right now."

"No, thanks. You've already done enough for me. That elbow tip is taking care of everything."

Tied 18th. Signed his card. Nicklaus signed mine. A 74. One of lowest scores in life. On one of world's hardest courses. Hard to believe, but true. Three handicap. Why not? Would look good out at Wildwood on the handicap sheet. Championship Flight. Would buy a new bag. Softer colors. Maybe new clothes. Probably talk less and be more modest. People would say, "That one, he's a 3." "Yeah, he looks like a 3. There's something about them."

"We waited all winter to find out that we're worse
this spring than we were last fall."

THE COMING OF GOWF

by P. G. WODEHOUSE

Prologue

After we had sent in our card and waited for a few hours in the marbled anteroom, a bell rang and the majordomo, parting the priceless curtains, ushered us in to where the editor sat writing at his desk. We advanced on all fours, knocking our heads reverently on the Aubusson carpet.

"Well?" he said at length, laying down his jeweled pen.

"We just looked in," we said humbly, "to ask if it would be all right if we sent you an historical story."

"The public does not want historical stories," he said, frowning coldly.

"Ah, but the public hasn't seen one of ours!" we replied.

The editor placed a cigarette in a holder presented to him by a reigning monarch and lit it with a match from a golden box, the gift of a millionaire president of the Amalgamated League of Working Plumbers.

"What this magazine requires," he said, "is red-blooded, 100 percent dynamic stuff, palpitating with warm human interest and containing a strong, poignant love motive."

"That," we replied, "is us all over, Mabel."

"What I need at the moment, however, is a golf story."

"By a singular coincidence, ours is a golf story."

"Ha! Say you so?" said the editor, a flicker of interest passing over his finely chiseled features. "Then you may let me see it."

He kicked us in the face, and we withdrew.

The Story

On the broad terrace outside his palace, overlooking the fair expanse of the Royal gardens, King Merolchazzar of Oom stood leaning on the low parapet, his chin in his hand and a frown on his noble face. The day was fine, and a light breeze bore up to him from the garden below a fragrant scent of flowers. But, for all the pleasure it seemed to give him, it might have been bone fertilizer.

The fact is, King Merolchazzar was in love, and his suit was

117

not prospering. Enough to upset any man.

Royal love affairs in those days were conducted on the correspondence system. A monarch, hearing good reports of a neighboring princess, would dispatch messengers with gifts to her court, beseeching an interview. The princess would name a date, and a formal meeting would take place, after which everything usually buzzed along pretty smoothly. But in the case of King Merolchazzar's courtship of the Princess of the Outer Isles there had been a regrettable hitch. She had acknowledged the gifts, saying that they were just what she wanted and how had he guessed and had added that, as regarded a meeting, she would let him know later. Since that day no word had come from her, and a gloomy spirit prevailed in the capital. At the Courtiers' Club, the meeting place of the aristocracy of Oom, 5 to 1 in pazazas was freely offered against Merolchazzar's chances, but found no takers; while in the taverns of the common people, where less conservative odds were always to be had, you could get a snappy 12 to 1. "For in good sooth," writes a chronicler of the time on a half-brick and a couple of paving stones which have survived to this day, "it did indeed begin to appear as though our beloved monarch, the son of the sun and the nephew of the moon, had been handed the bitter fruit of citron."

The quaint old idiom is almost untranslatable, but one sees what he means.

As the king stood somberly surveying the garden, his attention was attracted by a small, bearded man with bushy eyebrows and a face like a walnut, who stood not far away on a graveled path flanked by rosebushes. For some minutes he eyed this man in silence, then he called to the Grand Vizier, who was standing in the little group of courtiers and officials at the other end of the terrace. The bearded man, apparently unconscious of the Royal scrutiny, had placed a round stone on the gravel and was standing beside it, making curious passes over it with his hoe. It was this singular behavior that had attracted the king's attention. Superficially it seemed silly, and yet Merolchazzar had a curious feeling that there was a deep, even a holy, meaning behind the action.

"Who," he inquired, "is that?"

"He is one of Your Majesty's gardeners," replied the vizier.

"I don't remember seeing him before. Who is he?"

The vizier was a kind-hearted man, and he hesitated for a moment.

"It seems a hard thing to say of anyone, Your Majesty," he replied, "but he is a Scotsman. One of Your Majesty's invincible admirals recently made a raid on the inhospitable coast of that country at a spot known to the natives as S'nandrews and brought away this man."

"What does he think he's doing?" asked the king, as the bearded one slowly raised the hoe above his right shoulder, slightly bending the left knee as he did so.

"It is some species of savage religious ceremony, Your Majesty. According to the admiral, the dunes by the seashore where he landed were covered with a multitude of men behaving just as this man is doing. They had sticks in their hands and they struck with these at small round objects. And every now and again—."

"Fo-o-ore!" called a gruff voice from below.

"And every now and again," went on the vizier, "they would utter the strange melancholy cry which you have just heard. It is a species of chant."

The vizier broke off. The hoe had descended on the stone, and the stone, rising in a graceful arc, had sailed through the air and fallen within a foot of where the king stood.

"Hi!" exclaimed the vizier.

The man looked up.

"You mustn't do that! You nearly hit his Serene Graciousness, the King!"

"Mphm!" said the bearded man nonchalantly as he began to wave his hoe mystically over another stone.

Into the king's careworn face there had crept a look of interest, almost of excitement.

"What god does he hope to propitiate by these rites?" he asked.

"The deity, I learn from Your Majesty's admiral, is called Gowf."

"Gowf? Gowf?" King Merolchazzar ran over in his mind the muster roll of the gods of Oom. There were 67 of them, but Gowf was not of their number. "It is a strange religion," he murmured. "A strange religion, indeed. But, by Belus, distinctly attractive. I have an idea that Oom could do with a religion like that. It has zip to it. A sort of fascination, if you know what I mean. It looks to me extraordinarily like what the court physician ordered. I will talk to this fellow and learn more of these holy ceremonies."

And, followed by the vizier, the king made his way into the garden. The vizier was now in a state of some apprehension. He was exercised in his mind as to the effect which the embracing of a new religion by the king might have on the formidable church party. It would be certain to cause displeasure among the priesthood; and in those days it was a ticklish business to offend the priesthood, even for a monarch. And, if Merolchazzar had a fault, it was a tendency to be a little tactless in his dealings with that powerful body. Only a few mornings back the High Priest of Hec had taken the vizier aside to complain about the quality of the meat which the king had been using lately for his sacrifices. He might be a child in worldly matters, said the high priest, but if the king supposed that he did not know the difference between home-grown domestic and frozen imported foreign, it was time His

Majesty was disabused of the idea. If, on top of this little unpleasantness, King Merolchazzar were to become an adherent of this new Gowf, the vizier did not know what might not happen.

The king stood beside the bearded foreigner, watching him closely. The second stone soared neatly onto the terrace. Merolchazzar uttered an excited cry. His eyes were glowing and he breathed quickly.

"It doesn't look difficult," he muttered.

"Hoo's!" said the bearded man.

"I believe I could do it," went on the king, feverishly. "By the eight green gods of the mountain, I believe I could! By the holy fire that burns night and day before the altar of Belus, I'm sure I could! By Hec, I'm going to do it now! Gimme that hoe!"

"Toots!" said the bearded man.

It seemed to the king that the fellow spoke derisively and his blood boiled angrily. He seized the hoe and raised it above his shoulder, bracing himself solidly on widely parted feet. His pose was an exact reproduction of the one in which the court sculptor had depicted him when working on the life-size statue ("Our Athletic King") which stood in the principal square of the city; but it did not impress the stranger. He uttered a discordant laugh.

"Ye puir gonuph," he cried, "whitkin' o' a staunce is that?"

The king was hurt. Hitherto the attitude had been generally admired.

"It's the way I always stand when killing lions," he said. " 'In killing lions,' " he added, quoting from the well-known treatise of Nimrod, the recognized textbook on the sport, " 'the weight at the top of the swing should be evenly balanced on both feet.' "

"Ah, weel, ye're no killing lions the noo. Ye're gowfing."

A sudden humility descended upon the king. He felt, as so many men were to feel in similar circumstances in ages to come, as though he were a child looking eagerly for guidance to an all-wise master—a child, moreover, handicapped by water on the brain, feet three sizes too large for him and hands consisting mainly of thumbs.

"O thou of noble ancestors and agreeable disposition!" he said humbly. "Teach me the true way."

"Use the interlocking grup and keep the staunce a wee bit open and slow back, and dinna press or sway the heid and keep yer e'e on the ba'."

"My which on the what?" said the king, bewildered.

"I fancy, Your Majesty," hazarded the vizier, "that he is respectfully suggesting that your Serene Graciousness should deign to keep your eye on the ball."

"Oh, ah!" said the King.

The first golf lesson in the kingdom of Oom had begun.

"You were right, Emily . . . I've been a fool."

"First it was my marriage. Now the magic has gone out of my putter."

Upon the terrace, meanwhile, in the little group of courtiers and officials, a whispered consultation was in progress. Officially, the king's unfortunate love affair was supposed to be a strict secret. But you know how it is. These things get about. The Grand Vizier tells the Lord High Chamberlain; the Lord High Chamberlain whispers it in confidence to the Supreme Hereditary Custodian of the Royal Pet Dog; the Supreme Hereditary Custodian hands it on to the Exalted Overseer of the King's Wardrobe on the understanding that it is to go no further; and, before you know where you are, the varlets and scurvy knaves are gossiping about it in the kitchens and the society journalists have started to carve it out on bricks for the next issue of Palace Prattlings.

"The long and short of it is," said the Exalted Overseer of the King's Wardrobe, "we must cheer him up."

There was a murmur of approval. In those days of easy executions it was no light matter that a monarch should be a prey to gloom.

"But how?" queried the Lord High Chamberlain.

"I know," said the Supreme Hereditary Custodian of the Royal Pet Dog. "Try him with the minstrels."

"Here! Why us?" protested the leader of the minstrels.

"Don't be silly!" said the Lord High Chamberlain. "It's for your good just as much as ours. He was asking only last night why he never got any music nowadays. He told me to find out whether you supposed he paid you simply to eat and sleep, because if so he knew what to do about it."

"Oh, in that case!" The leader of the minstrels started nervously. Collecting his assistants and tiptoeing down the garden, he took up his stand a few feet in Merolchazzar's rear, just as that much-enduring monarch, after 25 futile attempts, was once more addressing his stone.

Lyric writers in those days had not reached the supreme pitch of excellence which has been produced by modern musical comedy. The art was in its infancy then, and the best the minstrels could do was this—and they did it just as Merolchazzar, raising the hoe with painful care, reached the top of his swing and started down:

> "Oh, tune the string and let us sing,
>   Our godlike, great and glorious King!
>   He's a bear! He's a bear! He's a bear!"

There were 16 more verses, touching on their ruler's prowess in the realms of sport and war, but they were not destined to be sung on that circuit. King Merolchazzar jumped like a stung bullock, lifted his head and missed the globe for the 26th time. He spun around on the minstrels, who were working pluckily through their song of praise:

> "Oh, may his triumphs never cease!
>   He has the strength of ten!
>   First in war, first in peace,
>   First in the hearts of his countrymen."

"Get out!" roared the King.

"Your Majesty?" quavered the leader of the minstrels.

"Make a noise like an egg and beat it!" (Again one finds the chronicler's idiom impossible to reproduce in modern speech and must be content with a literal translation.) "By the bones of my ancestors, it's a little hard! By the beard of the sacred goat, it's tough! What in the name of Belus and Hec do you mean, you yowling misfits, by starting that sort of stuff when a man's swinging? I was just shaping to hit it right that time when you butted in, you—."

The minstrels melted away. The bearded man patted the fermenting monarch paternally on the shoulder.

"Ma mannie," he said, "ye may no' be a gowfer yet, but hoots! Ye're learning the language fine!"

King Merolchazzar's fury died away. He simpered modestly at these words of commendation, the first his bearded preceptor had uttered. With exemplary patience he turned to address the stone for the 27th time.

That night it was all over the city that the king had gone crazy over a new religion, and the orthodox shook their heads.

We of the present day, living in the midst of a million marvels of a complex civilization, have learned to adjust ourselves to conditions and to take for granted phenomena which in an earlier and less advanced age would have caused the profoundest excitement and even alarm. We accept without comment the telephone, the automobile and the wireless telegraph, and we are unmoved by the spectacle of our fellow human beings in the grip of the first stages of golf fever. Far otherwise was it with the courtiers and officials about the Palace of Oom. The obsession of the king was the sole topic of conversation.

Everyday now, starting forth at dawn and returning only with the falling of darkness, Merolchazzar was out on the Linx, as the outdoor temple of the new god was called. In a luxurious house adjoining this expanse, the bearded Scotsman had been installed, and there he could be found at almost any hour of the day fashioning out of holy wood the weird implements indispensable to the new religion. As a recognition of his services, the king had bestowed upon him a large pension, innumerable kaddiz or slaves, and the title of Promoter of the King's Happiness, which for the sake of convenience was generally shortened to The Pro.

At present, Oom being a conservative country, the worship of the new god had not attracted the public in great numbers. In fact, except for the Grand Vizier, who, always a faithful follower of his sovereign's fortunes, had taken to Gowf from the start, the courtiers held aloof to a man. But the vizier had thrown himself into the new worship with such vigor and earnestness that it was not long before he won from the king the title of Supreme Splendiferous Maintainer of the 24 Handicap Except on Windy Days When It Goes Up to 30—a title which in ordinary conversation was usually abbreviated to The Dub.

All these new titles, it should be said, were, so far as the courtiers were concerned, a fruitful source of discontent. There were black looks and mutinous whispers. The laws of precedence were being disturbed, and the courtiers did not like it. It jars a man who for years has had his social position all cut and dried— a man, to take an instance at random, who, as Second Deputy Shiner of the Royal Hunting Boots, knows that his place is just below the Keeper of the Eel-Hounds and just above the Second Tenor of the Corps of Minstrels—it jars him, we say, to find suddenly that he has got to go down a step in favor of the Hereditary Bearer of the King's Baffy.

But it was from the priesthood that the real, serious opposition was to be expected. And the priests of the 67 gods of Oom were up in arms. As the white-bearded High Priest of Hec, who by virtue of his office, was generally regarded as leader of the guild, remarked in a glowing speech at an extraordinary meeting of the Priests' Equity Association, he had always set his face against the principle of the Closed Shop hitherto, but there were moments when every thinking man had to admit that enough was sufficient, and it was his opinion that such a moment had now arrived. The cheers which greeted the words showed how correctly he had voiced popular sentiment.

Of all those who had listened to the high priest's speech, none had listened more intently than the king's half-brother, Ascobaruch. A sinister, disappointed man, this Ascobaruch, with mean eyes and a crafty smile. All his life he had been consumed with ambition, and until now it had looked as though he must go to his grave with this ambition unfulfilled. All his life he had wanted to be King of Oom, and now he began to see daylight. He was sufficiently versed in court intrigues to be aware that the priests were the party that really counted, the source from which all successful revolutions sprang. And of all the priests the one that mattered most was the venerable High Priest of Hec.

It was to this prelate, therefore, that Ascobaruch made his way at the close of the proceedings. The meeting had dispersed after passing a unanimous vote of censure on King Merolchazzar, and the high priest was refreshing himself in the vestry—for the meeting had taken place in the Temple of Hec—with a small milk and honey.

"Some speech!" began Ascobaruch in his unpleasant, crafty

way. None knew better than he the art of appealing to human vanity.

The high priest was plainly gratified.

"Oh, I don't know," he said, modestly.

"Yessir!" said Ascobaruch. "Considerable oration. What I can never understand is how you think up all these things to say. I couldn't do it if you paid me. The other night I had to propose the Visitors at the Old Alumni dinner of Oom University, and my mind seemed to go all blank. But you just stand up and the words come fluttering out of you like bees out of a barn. I simply cannot understand it. The thing gets past me."

"Oh, it's just a knack."

"A divine gift, I should call it."

"Perhaps you're right," said the high priest, finishing his milk and honey. He was wondering why he had never realized before what a capital fellow Ascobaruch was.

"Of course," went on Ascobaruch, "you had an excellent subject. I mean to say, inspiring and all that. Why, by Hec, even I —though, of course, I couldn't have approached your level—even I could have done something with a subject like that. I mean, going off and worshipping a new god no one has ever heard of. I tell you, my blood fairly boiled. Nobody has a greater respect and esteem for Merolchazzar than I have, but I mean to say, what! Not right, I mean, going off worshipping gods no one has ever heard of! I'm a peaceable man, and I've made it a rule never to mix in politics, but if you happened to say to me as we were sitting here, just as one reasonable man to another—if you happened to say, 'Ascobaruch, I think it's time that definite steps were taken,' I should reply frankly, 'My dear old high priest, I absolutely agree with you, and I'm with you all the way.' You might even go so far as to suggest that the only way out of the muddle was to assassinate Merolchazzar and start with a clean slate."

The high priest stroked his beard thoughtfully.

"I am bound to say I never thought of going quite so far as that."

"Merely a suggestion, of course," said Ascobaruch. "Take it or leave it. I shan't be offended. If you know a superior excavation, go to it. But as a sensible man—and I've always maintained that you are the most sensible man in the country—you must see that it would be a solution. Merolchazzar has been a pretty good king, of course. No one denies that. A fair general, no doubt, and a plus-one at lion-hunting. But, after all—look at it fairly—is life all battles and lion-hunting? Isn't there a deeper side? Wouldn't it be better for the country to have some good orthodox fellow who has worshipped Hec all his life and could be relied on to maintain the old beliefs—wouldn't the fact that a man like that was on the throne be likely to lead to more general prosperity? There are dozens of men of that kind simply waiting to be asked. Let us say, purely for purposes of argument, that you approached me. I should

125

"We might be losing our momentum.
We've dropped the last seven holes."

reply, 'Unworthy though I know myself to be of such an honor, I can tell you this. If you put me on the throne, you can bet your bottom pazaza that there's one thing that won't suffer, and that is the worship of Hec!' That's the way I feel about it."

The high priest pondered.

"O thou of unshuffled features but amiable disposition!" he said, "thy discourse soundeth good to me. Could it be done?"

"Could it!" Ascobaruch uttered a hideous laugh. "Could it! Arouse me in the night watches and ask me! Question me on the matter, having stopped me for that purpose on the public highway! What I would suggest—I'm not dictating, mind you; merely trying to help you out—what I would suggest is that you take that long, sharp knife of yours, the one you use for the sacrifices, and toddle out to the Linx—you're sure to find the king there; and just when he's raising that sacrilegious stick of his over his shoulder. . . ."

"O man of infinite wisdom," cried the high priest warmly, "verily hast thou spoken a fullness of the mouth!"

"Is it a wager?" said Ascobaruch.

"It is a wager!" said the high priest.

"That's that, then," said Ascobaruch. "Now, I don't want to be mixed up in any unpleasantness, so what I think I'll do while what you might call the preliminaries are being arranged is to go and take a little trip abroad somewhere. The Middle Lakes are pleasant at this time of year. When I come back, it's possible that all the formalities will have been completed, yes?"

"Rely on me, by Hec!" said the high priest grimly, as he fingered his weapon.

The high priest was as good as his word. Early on the morrow he made his way to the Linx and found the king holing-out on the second green. Merolchazzar was in high good humor.

"Greetings, O venerable one!" he cried jovially. "Hadst thou come a moment sooner, thou wouldst have seen me lay my ball dead—aye, dead as mutton, with the sweetest little half-mashie-niblick chip shot ever seen outside the sacred domain of S'nandrew, on whom"—he bared his head reverently—"be peace! In one under bogey did I do the hole—yea, and that despite the fact that, slicing my drive, I became ensnared in yonder undergrowth."

The high priest had not the advantage of understanding one word of what the king was talking about, but he gathered with satisfaction that Merolchazzar was pleased and wholly without suspicion. He clasped an unseen hand more firmly about the handle of his knife and accompanied the monarch to the next altar. Merolchazzar stooped and placed a small round white object on a little mound of sand. In spite of his austere views, the high priest, always a keen student of ritual, became interested.

"Why does Your Majesty do that?"

"I tee it up that it may fly the fairer. If I did not, then would it be apt to run along the ground like a beetle instead of soaring like a bird, and mayhap, for thou seest how rough and tangled is the grass before us, I should have to use a niblick for my second."

The high priest groped for his meaning.

"It is a ceremony to propitiate the god and bring good luck?"

"You might call it that."

The high priest shook his head.

"I may be old-fashioned," he said, "but I should have thought that, to propitiate a god, it would have been better to have sacrificed one of these kaddiz on his altar."

"I confess," replied the king, thoughtfully, "that I have often felt that it would be a relief to one's feelings to sacrifice one or two kaddiz, but The Pro for some reason or other has set his face against it." He swung at the ball and sent it forcefully down the fairway. "By Abe, the son of Mitchell," he cried, shading his eyes, "a bird of a drive! How truly is it written in the book of the prophet Vadun, 'The left hand applieth the force, the right doth but guide. Grip not, therefore, too closely with the right hand!' Yesterday I was pulling all the time."

The high priest frowned.

"It is written in the sacred book of Hec, Your Majesty, 'Thou shalt not follow after strange gods.' "

"Take thou this stick, o venerable one," said the king, paying no attention to the remark, "and have a shot thyself. True, thou art well-stricken in years, but many a man has so wrought that he was able to give his grandchildren a stroke a hole. It is never too late to begin."

The high priest shrank back, horrified. The king frowned.

"It is our royal wish," he said coldly.

The high priest was forced to comply. Had they been alone, it is possible that he might have risked all on one swift stroke with his knife, but by this time a group of kaddiz had drifted up and were watching the proceedings with that supercilious detachment so characteristic of them. He took the stick and arranged his limbs as the king directed.

"Now," said Merolchazzar, "slow back and keep your e'e on the ba'!"

A month later, Ascobaruch returned from his trip. He had received no word from the high priest announcing the success of the revolution, but there might be many reasons for that. It was with unruffled contentment that he bade his charioteer drive him to the palace. He was glad to get back, for after all a holiday is hardly a holiday if you have left your business affairs unsettled.

As he drove, the chariot passed a fair open space on the outskirts of the city. A sudden chill froze the serenity of Ascobaruch's mood. He prodded the charioteer sharply in the back.

"What is that?" he demanded, catching his breath.

All over the green expanse could be seen men in strange robes, moving to and fro in couples and bearing in their hands mystic wands. Some searched restlessly in the bushes, others were walking briskly in the direction of small red flags. A sickening foreboding of disaster fell upon Ascobaruch.

The charioteer seemed surprised at the question.

"Yon's the muneecipal linx," he replied.

"The what?"

"The muneecipal linx."

"Tell me, fellow, why do you talk that way?"

"Whitway?"

"Why, like that. The way you're talking."

"Hoots, mon!" said the charioteer. "His Majesty King Merol-chazzar—may his handicap decrease!—hae passit a law that a' his soobjects shall do it. Aiblins, 'tis the language spoken by The Pro, on whom be peace! Mphm!"

Ascobaruch sat back limply, his head swimming. The chariot drove on, till now it took the road adjoining the royal Linx. A wall lined a portion of this road and, suddenly, from behind this wall, there rent the air a great shout of laughter.

"Pull up!" cried Ascobaruch to the charioteer.

He had recognized that laugh. It was the laugh of Merol-chazzar.

Ascobaruch crept to the wall and cautiously poked his head over it. The sight he saw drove the blood from his face and left him white and haggard.

The king and the grand vizier were playing a foursome against The Pro and the High Priest of Hec, and the vizier had just laid the high priest a dead stymie.

Ascobaruch tottered to the chariot.

"Take me back," he muttered pallidly. "I've forgotten something!"

And so golf came to Oom, and with it prosperity unequalled in the whole history of the land. Everybody was happy. There was no more unemployment. Crime ceased. The chronicler repeatedly refers to it in his memoirs as the Golden Age. And yet there remained one man on whom complete felicity had not descended. It was all right while he was actually on the Linx, but there were blank, dreary stretches of the night when King Merolchazzar lay sleepless on his couch and mourned that he had nobody to love him.

Of course, his subjects loved him in a way. A new statue had been erected in the palace square, showing him in the act of getting out of casual water. The minstrels had composed a whole cycle of up-to-date songs, commemorating his prowess with the mashie. His handicap was down to 12. But these things are not all. A golfer needs a loving wife, to whom he can describe the day's

play through the long evenings. And this was just where Merolchazzar's life was empty. No word had come from the Princess
of the Outer Isles, and, as he refused to be put off with just-as-good
substitutes, he remained a lonely man.

But one morning, in the early hours of a summer day as he
lay sleeping after a disturbed night, Merolchazzar was awakened
by the eager hand of the Lord High Chamberlain, shaking his
shoulder.

"Now what?" said the king.

"Hoots, Your Majesty! Glorious news! The Princess of the
Outer Isles waits without—I mean wi'oot!"

The king sprang from his couch.

"A messenger from the princess at last!"

"Nay, sire, the princess herself—that is to say," said the Lord
Chamberlain, who was an old man and had found it hard to
accustom himself to the new tongue at his age, "her ain sel'! And
believe me, or rather, mind ah' telling ye," went on the honest man
joyfully, for he had been deeply exercised by his monarch's
troubles, "Her Highness is the easiest thing to look at these eyes
hae ever seen. And you can say I said it!"

"She is beautiful?"

"Your Majesty, she is, in the best and deepest sense of the
word, a pippin!"

King Merolchazzar was groping wildly for his robes.

"Tell her to wait!" he cried. "Go and amuse her. Ask her
riddles! Tell her anecdotes! Don't let her go. Say I'll be down in a
moment. Where in the name of Zoroaster is our imperial mesh-
knit underwear?"

A fair and pleasing sight was the Princess of the Outer Isles as
she stood on the terrace in the clear sunshine of the summer
morning, looking over the king's gardens. With her delicate little
nose she sniffed the fragrance of the flowers. Her blue eyes
roamed over the rosebushes, and the breeze ruffled the golden
curls about her temples. Presently a sound behind her caused her
to turn, and she perceived a godlike man hurrying across the
terrace pulling up a sock. And at the sight of him the princess'
heart sang within her like the birds in the garden.

"Hope I haven't kept you waiting," said Merolchazzar
apologetically. He, too, was conscious of a strange, wild exhila-
ration. Truly was this maiden, as his chamberlain had said,
noticeably easy on the eyes. Her beauty was as water in the desert,
as fire on a frosty night, as diamonds, rubies, pearls, sapphires
and amethysts.

"Oh, no!" said the princess, "I've been enjoying myself. How
passing beautiful are thy gardens, O King!"

"My gardens may be passing beautiful," said Merolchazzar
earnestly, "but they aren't half so passing beautiful as thine eyes. I
have dreamed of thee by night and by day, and I will tell the world

130

I was nowhere near it! My sluggish fancy came not within a 157 miles of the reality. Now let the sun dim his face and the moon hide herself abashed. Now let the flowers bend their heads and the gazelle of the mountains confess itself a cripple. Princess, your slave!"

And King Merolchazzar, with that easy grace so characteristic of royalty, took her hand in his and kissed it.

As he did so, he gave a start of surprise.

"By Hec!" he exclaimed. "What has thou been doing to thyself? Thy hand is all over little rough places inside. Has some malignant wizard laid a spell upon thee, or what is it?"

The princess blushed.

"If I make that clear to thee," she said, "I shall also make clear why it was that I sent thee no message all this long while. My time was so occupied, verily I did not seem to have a moment. The fact is, these sorenesses are due to a strange, new religion to which I and my subjects have but recently converted. And O that I might make thee also of the true faith! 'Tis a wondrous tale, My Lord. Some two moons back there was brought to my court by wandering pirates a captive of an uncouth race who dwell in the north. And this man has taught us—."

King Merolchazzar uttered a loud cry.

"By Tom, the son of Morris! Can this truly be so? What is thy handicap?"

The princess stared at him, wide-eyed.

"Truly this is a miracle! Art thou also a worshipper of the great Gowf?"

"Am I!" cried the king. "Am I!" He broke off. "Listen!"

From the minstrels' room high up in the palace there came the sound of singing. The minstrels were practicing a new paean of praise—words by the Grand Vizier, music by the High Priest of Hec—which they were to render at the next full moon at the banquet of the worshippers of Gowf. The words came clear and distinct through the still air:

> "Oh, praises let us utter
> To our most glorious King!
> It fairly makes you stutter
> To see him start his swing!
> Success attend his putter!
> And luck be with his drive!
> And may he do each hole in two,
> Although the bogey's five!"

The voices died away. There was a silence.

"If I hadn't missed a two-foot putt, I'd have done the long 15th in four yesterday," said the king.

"I won the Ladies' Open Championship of the Outer Isles last week," said the princess.

They looked into each other's eyes for a long moment. And then, hand in hand, they walked slowly into the palace.

The Epilogue

"Well?" we said anxiously.

"I like it," said the editor.

"Good egg!" we murmured.

The editor pressed a bell, a single ruby set in a fold of the tapestry upon the wall. The majordomo appeared.

"Give this man a purse of gold," said the editor, "and throw him out."

"Then I realized the wife was right. I hadn't been spending enough time with the kids."

"... Playing through ..."

"Greenies, skins and presses?"

JOHNNY MILLER AND THE FAT CITY FIVE

by BRENNAN QUINN

Fat City lies just west of Highway 99 in the central valley of northern California. Rand McNally and gas station attendants call it Stockton. The area's topography and reputation are identical—flat. A well-known San Francisco journalist calls it "the hotbed of absolutely nothing." Maybe. But you can't always believe people who live and work on metropolitan sidehill lies.

In the 1940's Fat City housed more ethnic groups and had more bars per capita than any city in the United States. That was the good news. For two decades following World War II the high school graduating classes went out into the world in thirds—a third to work, a third to college and a third to jail. While this was going on Ben Hogan shot 71 here. Babe Zaharias shot 73. Gene Littler, fresh out of the Navy, won perhaps his first money as a pro in the General Hilario Moncado Tournament. That's right, General Hilario Moncado Tournament. Ask Littler, I can't begin to explain it.

South of the tracks, at the end of Wilson Way next to the 99 Speedway and the drive-in movie, a prosperous businessman designed and built his own nine-hole course. It may be the best of its kind in the world. You play 18 holes from two sets of blocks. Doug Sanders has done it, but he'd rather talk about something else. Arnold Palmer and Jack Nicklaus haven't—but they've heard about it. The course record of 68 is held by two guys who don't live in Fat City but should, Billy Casper and Bob Rosburg. The nine-holer has been the spawning ground of some frustrating golf and some unique characters.

Through the 1950's and most of the 60's, being a character was out. For a while it appeared as if 200 million people were going to turn into identical doubleknit turkeys. Thankfully, the late 60's and 70's brought more latitude and individualism. Frantic attempts to recreate a simpler, more realistic past prompted a nostalgia craze. Long hair returned to the head. Bib overalls returned to the body. Bogart and the Bowery Boys returned to the mind. Bogart, of course, is dead. But what of the Bowery Boys? Not quite! Middle-aged and making wagers, enjoying cocktails or sandbagging unsuspecting victims, they have flourished for years, alive and well-to-do—in Fat City.

On a 70-degree valley morning a yellow Porsche Carrera slides into a parking space at the corner of Sutter and Lindsay. A handsome young blond, good haircut, wearing Sears' best, emerges and heads for the offices of a leasing company in the middle of the block. Three girls from the telephone building stare, thinking they know him. They decide he isn't Redford, Jagger or Campbell, and walk on. One looks at the rear license plate. No numbers but small stencil-sprayed makeshift letters—Johnny Miller.

"Oh, yeah, he's a golfer."

The other two shrug and tilt their heads, not knowing.

Miller has come to Fat City, between tour stops, at the invitation of a close personal friend known to his golfing cohorts as Zapatos. Zapatos is a very successful business executive. One look tells you that if he's a Mexican American, Lee Trevino is the King of Sweden. They talk briefly about disposing of another of the many cars Miller wins, their families, golf games and the course record on the nine-holer they'll play that afternoon. Three phone calls later, Zapatos and Miller are heading south on Sutter Street into an old section of town toward On Lock Sam's. The same San Francisco journalist mentioned earlier has called On Lock's one of the best Chinese restaurants anywhere. He's right. Zapatos treats his guest to a magnificent spread for eight that would feed 20, including a specialty called spun glass. That's right, spun glass. Ask Rose Wong, I can't begin to explain that, either. Zapatos introduces Miller to the luncheon guests and afternoon's players—Hershey, Bince, Axehandle and Googie. Miller can't believe the characters or the cuisine, and the characters can't believe how much Miller can eat.

Later Axehandle will say, "The kid's amazing—eats like a python with manners."

Conversation is lively with the exception of Miller and Hershey. Miller is normally quiet and today he couldn't get a word past the wonton or sweet and sour.

In an hour and a half, Hershey says, "Boy, am I tired today"—four times.

During lunch some games are set. No big money, $2 four ways, automatic presses at 2 down. As Miller forks the last prawn, he nods at Zapatos. "Tell me what I owe at sundown."

They leave for the nine-holer where six golf cars are waiting.

In the parking lot Miller asks Zapatos how much the lunch cost.

"Don't worry about it," retorts his friend. "You couldn't afford it."

Miller laughs out loud.

The Fat City Five has an interesting and lucrative approach to golf. No one has a handicap under 10 or over 14. These numbers have raised eyebrows and ire in most of the 50 states and several foreign countries. But there is also an unwritten code—an ethic. They can have a hell of a time, three of them against a pro and a good amateur, no handicaps, best ball for $10. Usually at the end you shake for a drink and nobody pays. However, if you think you can play golf or cards for big bread, bring your confidence, cash and clubs to Fat City.

At the first tee Miller is introduced to things he has never seen on tour and never will. Hershey and Bince hit simultaneously. Hershey is a lefty. Both tee shots hook, crossing in the air but staying in the fairway. Miller's expression resembles that of a little kid at an air show. Hershey has teed off five feet in front of the blocks and nobody seems to care. Axehandle and Googie are next. Axe hits a hook as Googie gets a little left to right. Again Miller is treated to golf's answer to the Thunderbirds. A possible crisscross hat trick is avoided as Zapatos gestures Miller to the tee. He looks and feels alone. He sets, three quick waggles and hits a very adequate tee shot down the right center.

"That'll do," says Hershey who hasn't seen the shot, apparently captivated by one of his favorite weapons, the ball washer. Before Miller picks up his tee, Zapatos has hit. By the time Miller straightens up the entire group is halfway down the fairway. It's undoubtedly the first time in history a U.S. Open champion has played in a sixsome and felt alone—twice—on the first tee.

Miller's candor is refreshing, "Would you look at those shots and everyone in the fairway."

He's addressing one of the perhaps 10 people watching. Miller moves along conversing with an onlooker until interrupted.

"How can I concentrate on my game with all this talking goin' on?"

It's Hershey.

"Excuse me," says Miller.

"That's better," replies Hershey, chuckling at his own material and hitting a long iron at the same time.

The ball, hit low on the club, makes an odd thonking sound but winds its way to the apron and bounces to rest about six feet from the hole.

Googie states a truth, "Hersh is the only golfer in the world who can work a brand new Top-Flite left to right to left."

Three players hit the green, three miss. Miller is 12 feet past the hole. His putt slides by. Hershey asks Miller to line up his short birdie putt.

"The last time I said anything you told me to shut up," says the Open champion.

"But we're partners," Hershey tells him in a phony pleading tone.

"Straight in!" says Miller.

Hershey sinks it. One birdie, four pars and one bogey. Not bad when you consider the total handicap of the sixsome is 58 and one of the players doesn't own one.

Miller becomes intrigued by the Fat City Five—you can't help it. They are a little bit like a demolition derby, almost impossible to explain but great fun to watch.

Miller's host, Zapatos, is an immaculate casual dresser, favoring pastels from collar to spikes. He can chew gum like an infielder, talk faster than an auctioneer, chip like a wizard and do a reasonable impression of a human walk. Zapatos has to be considered one of the best pro-am players alive. Standing next to Miller, he could pass for a fellow professional. This thought is dispelled as he addresses the ball using the same grip King Arthur did when he pulled the sword from the stone in Camelot. Years of chronic back trouble have left the swing with an orthopedic quickness. Occasionally, when the peacock is pumped up he plays unbelievable golf. Walking off the tee he resembles a large-framed Pancho Segura breaking in a pair of corrective Foot-Joys.

Hershey, born tired and left-handed, has faced life straight while yawning his way through half a century plus. Although his handicap is 11, it is not unusual for Hersh to hit 14 to 16 greens per round—with his golf car. Hersh believes in getting down to the ball, never starting his swing until both hands are well below his knees and the toe of the club is pointing at the moon.

Miller called him "the only golfer I've ever seen with green knuckles."

Hershey has not played a single hole since the Korean War without hitting out of turn at least once.

Bince's specialty is changing an X shaft to a ladies' whippy simply by practice swinging. Nicklaus tightens his grip slightly and rotates his head to trigger the swing. Bince, who is short and burly, uses his strength to begin the swing by pushing down severely with his hands and forcing the club shaft into the configuration of a Zen archer's bow. The shaft, not Bince, springs the rapid slash into being. Maximum foot action is utilized.

The finish reminds one of a Russian circus bear dribbling a beach ball with his paw. Bince turns the most expensive golf shoes into imitation alligator tortillas in a week. He also can throw a pitching wedge 75 yards and has spent two decades attempting to find a use for the god-awful thing. His clubs appear to have been acquired at Harry Vardon's estate sale. But don't be fooled. If anybody discovers a way to turn fertilizer into strawberry short-cake, it will probably be Bince.

Axehandle stands to the ball the way Joe Namath sets behind center—round back and straight legs, but Axe seldom if ever wears pantyhose. Axe can't rotate his head to initiate the swing as God didn't provide him with a neck. Bince says his extremely rugged appearance was forged long ago when, on 17 separate and distinct occasions, he called Tony Galento a dumb wop! (Bince has never been mistaken for Marcello Mastroianni.) Axehandle can make beautiful furniture and sink putts, as if by magic, around Hershey's feet. He can play golf in the 70's with a Bob Murphy hat pulled down completely obscuring his vision. Recently Axe shot 69 in a tournament and immediately changed clubs. This surprised no one, being standard procedure on Tuesday, Friday and Sunday, regardless of performance.

Googie is a gentleman farmer and stock market buff accused erroneously of retiring before his father did. A graduate of one of the finest universities in the country, Googie has deftly managed to completely disguise the fact. He always hits with a cigarette in his mouth a la Lloyd Mangrum. The swing starts when the inch-long ash falls from the dangling roach. Googie plays his best golf when the ash falls somewhere between his arms. His arsenal includes seven woods and assorted irons. All head covers with numbers are carefully placed on the wrong clubs. Any shot over 12 feet high is skied. On or off the course Googie is the world's foremost authority on why things that should have happened didn't. Googie's mark is a half-smoked Camel, still burning, somewhere on every green he ever played.

On the third tee Miller inquires about the hole.

"Three par," says Zapatos, teeing up his 1-wood.

Miller waits as everybody hits drivers. All are short with the exception of Axehandle who hits a blue darter six feet onto the front of the green. The junkmen have totally confused Miller. Someone watching suggests that it's a minimum of 245 yards to the hole. Miller isn't sure. He hits a beautiful looking 3-wood that blanks out the flag but comes to rest three feet in front of Axe-handle's ball—80 feet short.

"Whoo-ee that's some hole."

"That isn't very good for a pro," offers the ever-charitable Hershey.

On the next par 3, No. 6, Miller lets a 4-iron slip right of the green and leaves himself a very difficult pitch. Googie is the only player to hit the green, using an unidentified flying wooden club. Miller hits a beautiful soft lob three feet past the hole and makes the putt. This professional recovery is somewhat dimmed by the fact that Zapatos and Bince both chip in for 2's.

As they head for the seventh tee Miller's candor surfaces again. "These guys are too much. I thought there were some good short games on the tour. You know, some of those guys out there don't hit the ball all that well but they can really get it up and down." He names a couple. "But not like this. I hit a lot of greens and the short game suffers. I've got the worst short game in this group."

When the day is over Miller has hit a fence, a lake, missed several makable putts, played some superb golf and shot 72. The owner of the course appears from his house as the group hits second shots on the last hole.

"How we doing?"

"Birdie for 71," answers Zapatos.

They retire to the clubhouse. Relaxing with a Seven-Up, Miller does some quick arithmetic.

"Let's see, the best I did was with you, Googie, you only beat me 6 up. The only one of you guys I would consider playing at handicap is Bince and only then at the Olympic Club, from the back tees, in a driving rainstorm."

"Not until you can play better," suggests Hershey.

No money changes hands, it's getting late, a gin game has started. Miller says goodbye and heads for his little yellow car. He drives slowly down the private road peering at the nine-holer in the twilight. He vows to return and bring the mini-monster to its knees. At the large gate he turns left toward Highway 99, reminding himself to keep his speed close to his scoring average—which has been a problem in the past.

"Strange, six hours have gone by and I'm not hungry."

He catches 99 North.

"Boy, I hope that guy never agrees to that offer in the rain."

"That's the only time all day poor Ed's put two shots together."

"How about a side bet for low gross on lost balls?"

"As long as his clubs fit in the trunk,
he doesn't care about miles per gallon."

THE ASTOUNDING STORY OF THE GOLFING GORILLAS

by K. JASON SITEWELL

I have a Danish friend who is the director of the Royal Copen-hagen zoo—one of the world's best. About 10 years ago my friend came to the United States on a tour of American zoos. He was especially impressed with the show the gorillas and chimpanzees put on at the St. Louis zoo—riding motorcycles and doing circus acts. My friend hired the young assistant trainer at the St. Louis zoo and brought him to Copenhagen for the purpose of developing a chimpanzee-and-gorilla act that would be a prime tourist attraction.

My friend succeeded. Within three years the primates at the Royal Copenhagen zoo could put on a performance that was unsurpassed anywhere in the world. Not even the St. Louis zoo could match it. Chimpanzees did high-wire acts, typed words called out by people in the audience and played the guitar. One gorilla executed a perfect reverse two-and-a-half twist from the high diving board.

Three years ago, I visited my zoo-keeping Danish friend. The next day we played golf at the Royal Deer Park Golf Course just outside Copenhagen. He has a 7-handicap and plays several times a week. As usually happens, we traded golf stories and I was surprised to discover he hadn't heard the oldie about the golf-playing gorilla.

I am almost embarrassed to repeat it here. Anyway, it seems that a golf-playing gorilla was brought out to the local country club to test his skill in an actual game. The first hole, a par-5, was 550 yards. The gorilla hit his drive straight down the middle—285 yards. His fairway shot was good for 265 yards and rolled to within 20 feet of the cup. The gorilla's putt was a beauty—260 yards before it even hit the ground.

My friend didn't laugh. His mouth dropped open and he stared off into the distance like a character in a comic strip just before an electric bulb lights up over his head indicating he has just been hit with a hot idea.

"What is it?" I asked.

"That story is not as far-fetched as you might think," he said. "Why shouldn't a gorilla be able to play golf? I'm going to talk to my trainer right away. If we can bring this off, it will be the greatest gorilla act of all time. We'll make history."

He pledged me to secrecy because he wanted the Royal Copenhagen zoo to be the first to boast of a golf-playing gorilla.

His trainer fell in with the idea. They worked with the brightest young gorilla in the primate house. They started with a shortened polo mallet and an oversized softball. Then gradually they lengthened the club, reducing the size of both the clubhead and the ball.

For the first month or so the gorilla would lunge wildly at the ball, like a drunk swinging a broom at a bumblebee. But, little by little, the trainer was able to get the gorilla to shorten his swing. After about four months of steady work, the gorilla developed a fairly controlled swing, although he had a marked tendency to sway.

Then after another three months of daily training, the gorilla showed surprising progress. He learned to keep from swaying and to keep his head still. The best clubweight for the gorilla was an H6—or about twice the headweight of the average club.

The gorilla finally mastered a short backswing—not quite as short as Doug Sanders', but short enough. What really excited my friend and the trainer was the gorilla's wrist action. This was something he didn't have to be taught. Those wrists would snap just right as he came into the ball.

It took about a year and a half of solid day-in-and-day-out training before my friend was confident enough to bring the gorilla out to the Royal Deer Park Course. After a few holes my friend couldn't have been more elated. The experiment was working out beautifully. The gorilla, dressed in Gene Sarazen knickers and an orange-striped blazer, quickly demonstrated his aptitude. While he didn't get the fantastic distance of the gorilla in the story, he did manage to hit about 190-200 yards. The shots were occasionally erratic but not more so than those of the average bogey player.

The fairway shots tended to be more troublesome than the others. Not having the ball teed up was a problem. Sometimes the gorilla would top the ball and just about shear off a piece of it. And the divots, when he hit under the ball, were not to be believed— huge clumps of earth the size of one of Pearl Bailey's wigs and weighing about two pounds. But the clubhead made contact with the ball just the same.

What was truly astounding was that, unlike the gorilla in the story, the Copenhagen gorilla had no difficulty with his putting. In fact, this was the best part of his game. He had the advantage of being able to lie flat on his stomach behind the ball in lining up the pathway to the cup. He had a good sense of distance and knew how to make allowances for the varying conditions of different greens.

Unlike most players, the gorilla was not psyched out once he took a putter in his hands. In the first full game he played, he had only two three-putt greens on the round.

My friend toted up the score at the end of 18 holes—103 strokes, not bad considering it was the gorilla's first time out.

Subsequently, they were able to knock about 10 strokes off the gorilla's score by improving his fairway game.

My friend had succeeded. The number of visitors to the Royal Copenhagen zoo increased by 60 percent. The gorilla's act was very simple. Instead of using expensive golf balls, the trainer had the gorilla hit Ping-Pong balls directly at the delighted audience. Then the gorilla would put on a demonstration of putting. The floor was covered with an Astroturf circular carpet about 25 feet in diameter. The crowds would go wild with enthusiasm when the gorilla dropped putts of 12 feet or more.

I wish I could say that this report has a happy ending. Unfortunately, neither my friend nor the trainer was able to anticipate the unusual turn their experiment was to take. They hadn't counted on the fact that the gorilla, having learned the game, would insist on playing almost every day. If he wasn't taken out to the Royal Deer Golf Course, he would refuse to eat and would moan most of the day. And even when they allowed him to play, he wasn't satisfied with 18 holes. He insisted on going on and would put up a terrible struggle when they tried to lead him back to the zoo's truck. He had to be tranquilized by injection just to get the golf club out of his hands.

Another unexpected development was that the gorilla became morose because his mate wasn't allowed to go with him to the golf course. Finally, it became necessary for the trainer to teach golf to the female gorilla, too. The female had her own ideas about the purpose of the game. The only part of golf that really seemed to appeal to her was making mammoth divots. She didn't even need the pretext of a golf ball on the fairway to launch an attack on the turf. She would hack away at will, letting out shrieks of joy with each clump of earth that spurted into the air.

I must not neglect to mention the fact that the gorillas had atrocious golf manners. They had a possessive feeling about the sport and resented humans using what they believed to be their own private playground. If there were golfers on the fairway in front of them, the gorillas had to be restrained from taking off after the players, brandishing their clubs to the accompaniment of savage shrieks.

Naturally, this was very disconcerting to the players, especially to those who were on the Royal Deer Park Course for the first time and unaware of the golf-playing gorillas. (I could imagine how the players must have felt—sizing up their fairway shots and settling over their ball, only to hear terrifying cries and then looking up at two gorillas bearing down on them flailing golf clubs.)

The addiction of the gorillas to golf made them almost suicidal if they missed a single day on the links. To cap it all, the female gorilla became pregnant. X-ray examination showed she was going to have twins. The zoo director and the trainer had a serious talk at this point. They could foresee what would happen. The parent gorillas would insist that their young go with them and play, too. It was bad enough the way it was, with the fairways being chewed up, two groundskeepers resigning and members of the club complaining about having to allow gorillas to play through. But a whole new generation of gorillas coming along was more than anyone could take.

The outcome was inevitable. The gorillas had to be shipped away to the government wildlife park in Kenya. It was a sad day —not just for the gorillas but for my friend and the trainer—when the creatures were loaded onto the truck. My friend could tell from the gorillas' eyes that the animals, who had been crying for a long time, knew that something terrible was about to happen. So my friend got both bags of golf clubs and put them in the packing cage.

Then, when the gorillas were tranquilized and loaded into the cage, my friend went up to them for his last look. The gorillas were huddled in opposite corners, each clinging to a bag of golf clubs.

My friend is not given to sentimentality, but he told me it was one of the most poignant scenes he had ever witnessed. And he felt guilty for having been responsible for the chain of events that had led to such a melancholy ending.

I told my friend that his feelings of guilt were nothing compared to my own, for I was the one who had told him the absurd story that got him started.

What happened to the gorillas after they arrived in Kenya? My friend says that they were allowed to keep the clubs, and they used up, in a couple of months, the four dozen balls stuffed into the pockets of the golf bag. Thereafter, the gorillas would swing at pieces of dried dung that abounded in the wildlife park, or they would hack away at the grasslands, making divots even larger than the ones that caused so much grief in Copenhagen.

This completes the story except for a brief footnote. During the three months before the gorillas left Copenhagen, a team of zoologists and anthropologists carefully studied the creatures. The proficiency of the gorillas in golf—the male, at least, scored consistently in the low 90's—could not be explained by anything known in science about the remarkable learning skills of gorillas or about the advanced teaching techniques of gorilla-training. The more the academicians observed films of the male gorilla playing golf, the more convinced they were that they were dealing with atavistic phenomena.

Their reluctant and final conclusion was that golf was a natural and almost instinctive activity with gorillas, a form of recreation that in one form or another was native to their ancestors.

The corollary, of course, is that the human species, in supporting the game, is actually engaging in a form of early ancestral worship.

What the scholars are saying, in effect, is that the gorillas didn't get golf from man, but that man got golf from gorillas. Fortunately, the scholars can't prove it. Just the same, I get a sinking feeling every time I think about it.

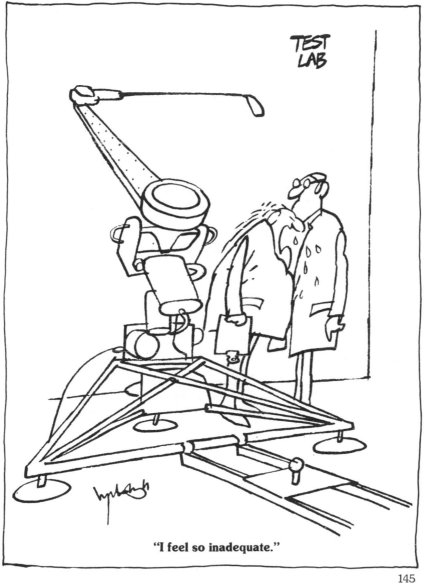

"I feel so inadequate."

HOW I BEAT THE WORLD'S GREATEST GOLFERS

by CHARLES BROME

A few minutes before shooting my legendary 55 at Winged Foot, I lined everybody up in the driveway for the official humming of the National Anthem. A little touch of class like that never hurts.

Some of the group apparently had never played championship golf in a garage before, and I could sense a certain amount of confusion. As the last discordant notes died away and the networks cut to a brief five-minute commercial, I invited questions.

Tom Weiskopf was the first to speak.

"How in the hell can we play Winged Foot in your crummy garage?" he growled. "And what in the hell is Walter Hagen doing here?"

I smiled. "I'm glad you had the courage to ask those questions, Tom," I said. "Never hesitate to ask questions, my boy. No matter how mutinous they may be, nor how dreadful the consequences."

Whereupon I turned Tom Weiskopf into Hubie Green.

"Well, Hubie," I explained, "it's like this. We can be at Winged Foot because I have the power to transpose my garage into any golf course I want it to be. And we actually can play the course because when I hit a ball into the net, here in the garage, I have the power to tell instantly what kind of shot it would have been."

Hubie nodded his understanding.

"And Walter is here," I continued, "for the same reason the rest of you are here. My mastery of the game is so complete that not only can I duplicate the swing of any golfer who ever lived, but I actually have the power to become that golfer. At the peak of his game, naturally."

There was a spattering of spontaneous applause at this. But from somewhere in the back, in unmistakably sarcastic tones, came a loud, "Oh, aye?"

Tommy Armour shouldered his way forward and fixed me with an icy stare.

"Oh, aye?" he repeated. "And how, may I ask, does one manage to acquire such miraculous bloody skills and such incredible bloody powers?"

146

More in sorrow than in anger, I turned Tommy Armour into Arnold Palmer.

Then, very patiently, I explained that there was nothing miraculous or incredible about it.

I had simply hung a net in the garage for winter practice and then dedicated the rest of my life to hitting balls into it. The resulting perfection, I explained modestly, was only to be expected, given my perhaps unique physical and mental gifts.

"Why Winged Foot, sir?" someone wanted to know. "That's pretty tough."

I explained my hope that the West Course there, juiced up the way it was for the U.S. Open a few years ago, might offer a suitable challenge for my skills.

"We'd hardly want some pitch-and-putt layout, would we?" I chided gently. "A course like Oakmont, where every Tom, Dick and Harry can shoot 63?"

"About the putts," Jack Nicklaus asked. "Won't they be too easy? The cement floor of this garage is at least 20 percent softer and a good bit slower than the greens at Winged Foot."

I agreed. But we need not bother with actually putting, I said. I would handle that part mentally.

Johnny Miller had been looking nervously at the garage rafters.

"Sir," he asked, after clearing his throat a few times, "aren't these rafters just a little bit lower than the ones at Winged Foot?"

Quite right, I told him. But since I intended to hit all shots with a cut-down Bobby Jones 5-iron, the rafters would not come into play.

Should the USGA wish to enshrine that soon-to-be-famous club in a glass case in Far Hills, N.J., I added casually, I would not object. Assuming an appropriate club enshrinement fee, of course.

By this time the commercial break was over and Walter Cronkite explained the official format for the match. The committee had decided that I was to compete against nine different players, he said, two holes each, for the All-Time Championship of the World.

Walter added that Joseph C. Dey had been summoned to act as referee, Davey Marr and Ken Venturi would do TV commentary and analysis. Herbert Warren Wind, using a special pencil, would write the numbers on the official scoreboard.

Formal opening ceremonies were simple and dignified.

We all hummed the National Anthem again, just for luck.

Joseph C. Dey sounded a blast on a golden trumpet.

Hubie Green hooked his drive into the deep rough, and the match was on!

I had selected Hubie as representative of the younger generation of golfers. Not yet in the same league with us mature players, perhaps, but a promising lad.

Nor was my confidence misplaced. Hubie did come a bit

147

heavily out of the rough, landing in a bunker short of the green. And he did blast out a trifle tentatively, to about 14 feet. But he then coolly holed a wicked putt for par.

I played the hole less raggedly. It is a relatively simple par 4 of only 446 yards, with bunkers left and right about 60 yards short of the green. A 3-wood off the tee put me safely short of the bunkers (I rarely allow myself to hit a 3-wood more than 380 yards, for fear of demolishing the net), leaving a routine wedge and a tap-in for birdie.

On the second hole I decided to attack. The hole is a trifling 411 yards in length, but it doglegs sharply to the right, and two deep bunkers make for a dangerously narrow opening to the green. The hole was cut at the extreme right, directly beneath the branches of a large tree.

The conservative tee shot would be an iron to the left edge of the fairway, thus insuring a reasonably safe approach. But I realized that a really strong drive down the left, provided it faded sharply exactly 300 yards out, would put me in birdie position.

Hubie's eyes widened when he saw me take out my driver, and I could hear Ken Venturi whispering excitedly into his mike.

"He's really going to have to jump all over the shot if he expects to keep it in the fairway with that club, Dave," he said.

"I'm afraid I am not at all sure just what that means, Ken," came back a moment later through the little plastic thing in his ear.

"I'm standing very close and can't talk now," Ken explained.

Flashing my famous devil-may-care smile, I teed the ball a hair higher than usual and swung. What the TV camera could not show, of course, was a secret movement of the big toe and the first little piggy on my right foot, a move which imparts 43 percent more power to the shot but should be used only in extreme situations because of the enormous mental control it demands.

Long and true the ball soared, upward and upward toward a spot at which the net was specially reinforced and there was also a large tree left of the fairway. Precisely at that spot the ball started to fade toward the green, more and more sharply until it disappeared behind the trees which blocked our view.

Ken Venturi listened intently to the thing in his ear for a moment. Then, with a touch of awe in his voice, he announced: "The ball is on the green, eight feet past the hole!"

Upon hearing this, Hubie Green fainted. But we threw some water on him and he eventually came to and bogeyed the hole.

I rapped in the putt for a routine eagle and was joined on the third tee by my next opponent, Byron Nelson.

"Nice shot you hit back there," he said amiably. "Right big toe and second little piggy?"

"First little piggy," I said.

He thought hard for a moment, then nodded approval. As the greatest golfer who ever lived, Byron Nelson is one of the few people in the world capable of understanding a move as secret as that one.

The third hole is a 216-yard par 3, downwind, with a long, skinny, nasty, hard, humpy green guarded at either side by yawning bunkers. The pin, naturally, was tucked in behind the deepest one.

I graciously offered Byron the honor and he stroked a lovely, high, soft 2-iron three feet from the hole. Just beautiful.

To this day, I still blush at my own shot. The crowd had roared its appreciation for Nelson's magnificent effort, and the TV people had taken five minutes to show it over and over in slow motion, stop-action and various combinations thereof.

Venturi explained how Byron had to jump all over the shot in order to get there with that club. Davey Marr pointed out that the shot proved that a smooth, easy swing always gets the best results.

On top of all those distractions, I was more than a little awed to be playing with Byron Nelson, who has always been my idol. Even if he did promise me a set of clubs once and then failed to deliver. He probably just forgot.

At any rate, by the time things calmed down enough for me to hit, my concentration was pretty well shot.

I had selected a 2-iron also (a 3-iron would have been plenty for me, but I didn't want to show up Byron). I gauged the precise force necessary to send the ball 216 yards, with routine modifications for the effects of wind, temperature and barometric pressure. Plus minor adjustments for a tiny imperfection in the ball and the fact that the top of the wooden tee had been unevenly painted.

But with all the excitement, I neglected to allow either for rotation of the earth or for the magnetic orientation of Winged Foot to the Great Pyramid.

Pure carelessness, of course, and the consequence should rightfully have been a shot a full inch and a half off line. Imagine my surprise, then, when the ball took two quick bounces and rolled directly into the hole!

As might be expected, a certain amount of hysteria took over when my ball rattled into the cup. The blonde lady who makes those shaving soap commercials broke through the ropes and flung herself at my feet, but missed. That sort of thing.

But I was far from pleased. In the first place, I could derive little satisfaction from holing out a shot I knew had been improperly planned. Worse yet, my birdie-eagle-ace start suggested that Winged Foot was simply incapable of providing the kind of challenge I had hoped for.

Nor did the next hole, a fairly easy 460-yard par 4, offer a lift for my spirits. Nelson drove the fairway, pushed a 1-iron into the bunker, blasted within inches of the cup and made par. I hit a 3-wood a few yards past Nelson's drive, then a 4-iron that looked for a ghastly moment as if it, too, were going into the hole.

149

"Now our past champion will hand over the
trophy . . . please hand over the trophy!"

Fortunately for my frame of mind, however, the ball stopped four feet short of the hole. I made the birdie putt, despite having to negotiate some spike marks Byron accidentally kicked up when he was seized with a leg cramp, or something.

"Nice putt," I heard someone say as I walked glumly over to the fifth tee. It was Ben Hogan, my next opponent.

"Yes, it was," I agreed, graciously autographing the program he held out. "But for a minute I was afraid that 4-iron was going into the hole and I wouldn't get to putt at all."

He shook his head. "It would have lipped out even if it had got up to the hole. As a matter of fact, that shot on No. 3 shouldn't have gone in either. You were lined up an inch and a quarter to the left."

"An inch and a half, I believe, Ben," I said, as gently as I could.

Even so, the correction irritated him, and we both birdied five and six in silence. Ben Hogan is the second greatest golfer who ever lived, next to Byron Nelson, but he invariably gets mad when I correct him on a point of golf. He always gets over it very quickly, though, and sends me a set of clubs.

The next two holes were more relaxed. I was paired with Arnold Palmer, which is always a pleasure, and he was his usual friendly self.

On the seventh (166 yards, par 3) we turned back into the wind. Arnie ripped a low 6-iron 20 feet past the hole and I rather foolishly hit a 7-iron. The ball got up into the wind and barely made the front edge of the green, perhaps 90 feet short of the cup. But I managed to drop the putt for birdie.

Arnie's downhill 20-footer was much, much too bold. The crowd moaned. Arnold grinned, hitched up his pants, squinted once at the line and rapped the ball squarely into the back of the hole for par—to the cheers of the multitude, myself included.

He saved par again on No. 8, holing a fine 18-foot putt after coming out of the sand a touch heavily, and I birdied from about 11 feet. As on the previous hole, the crowd went delirious over Arnie's lucky par, but paid no attention at all to my own brilliant play. But I didn't mind.

On the ninth tee I was greeted warmly by Sam Snead. Sam was the first player I had learned how to become, back in my early days. His swing is pretty much patterned after mine anyway, which made it easier. By this time we were fast friends.

"Care to risk a couple of bob?" he asked. Sam always likes to play for money, even in a friendly match. The last time we added it up, he owed me just under a hundred thousand dollars.

"Sure, Sam, if you want to," I said. "But I can't give you your usual stroke a hole in this kind of match, you know."

We agreed on a friendly $100,000 a hole, without strokes, and damned if Sam didn't hole out a 1-iron for an eagle on that monstrous 466-yard par 4, against the wind! The best I could do was birdie, which gave me a commendable 11-under-par 24 for the front nine, but left me actually owing money to Sam Snead!

Sam was quivering all over, he was so eager to get to the next tee. The 10th is a treacherous par 3 of 190 yards, all carry. That means a long iron, and when Sam Snead has a 2-iron in his hands, he fears not man or beast.

But I insisted that we take a moment to sit on the garden tractor and share a friendly glass of water and a cheese sandwich before we hit. I was getting $100,000 a minute for TV commercial time, and figured a few extra minutes couldn't hurt. Besides, I wanted to give Sam time to think about his shot.

It didn't work, though. He may possibly have been thinking about it. Maybe even worrying, for all I know. But once he made his forward press such things became academic. He made the same lovely swing he's been making for 40 years, and his ball landed as softly as a marshmallow, not 10 feet from the hole.

The wind was coming in gusts now, but I timed them nicely and drilled a low 2-iron that bit just past the flag and drew back to inside a foot. Sam's putt teetered on the lip and refused to fall. I tapped in for my 2 and was a hundred big ones in the black again. Sorry about that putt, Sam.

On the 11th tee there was a delay of nearly an hour while we waited for Walter Hagen to show up. He finally arrived, in an enormous limousine driven up by the Duke of Windsor.

The Haig was semi-resplendent in formal morning attire, which he had converted for golf by rolling up the pants legs and donning a pair of khaki puttees. From somewhere deep in the bowels of the limousine he produced a brace of English earls, one to carry his bag and one to hand him champagne between shots.

Personally, I thought the whole thing was a little much. But I did have to admit that he added a note of class to what had heretofore been a fairly nondescript garage.

I had purposely scheduled him for the 11th hole because although it is quite short (382 yards) it has the narrowest, bumpiest landing area in the world. I figured he was bound to miss the fairway, thus giving me a chance to watch one of the famous Hagen recovery shots from the wilderness.

But I had underestimated my man. With magnificent disdain, Hagen ignored the 11th fairway completely! Instead, he set up to hit some 30 degrees to the right, swayed nonchalantly through the shot and sent a tremendous drive sailing clear over the wilderness to the center of the 18th fairway, exactly 165 yards from the 11th green.

From there he arched a towering mashie shot that cleared a tree by less than a foot and a greenside bunker by less than six inches. The ball came to rest on the lip of the hole.

Hagen chuckled.

"Can't sink 'em all," he said, and went whistling off to the next tee.

Meanwhile, I had driven far past the normal landing area to the only flat place on the fairway, hit a crisp 8-iron to four feet and made birdie myself.

But nobody noticed. They were all over at the 12th tee where Hagen was handing out orchids to the lady spectators.

No. 12, at 535 yards, is the longest hole on the course. It dog-legs hard to the left, the fairway slopes sharply to the right in the landing area, and the narrow entrance to the green is guarded by a pair of those bottomless pits they use for bunkers at Winged Foot.

Even with a new net, I would normally hesitate to go for that green in two. But not Hagen. He put everything he had into his drive, a Herculean blast that hooked just enough to hug the slope and get every inch of roll possible. At the very end it bumped off to the right and trickled into the rough.

I used my secret move again and split the fairway, some 20 yards past his ball.

Until then, Hagen had more or less ignored me. But now he walked over and thrust out his hand.

"I'm going to beat you, whoever you are," he declared. "But by golly, when a man hits 10 yards past my best shot I want to shake his hand."

I was flattered, naturally. But I was also aware that an intense competitor like Hagen would try to turn my good shot to his own advantage.

And, sure enough, as we walked arm-in-arm down the fairway, he added in the friendliest way imaginable, "It'd be a damned shame to mess up your second shot after a drive like that, wouldn't it? Try not to think about it."

I just smiled. I smiled again when we reached his ball and he asked in a very loud voice for his brassie. There was no way he was going to try to hit a brassie out of that rough, and we both knew it.

But I was wrong. Hagen examined his lie minutely, even going so far as to check beneath the mat to be sure the garage floor was perfectly smooth. Then he slicked back his hair, winked at a comely female person in the gallery and flailed away with his wooden club.

The ball exploded from the high grass like a bullet. Low and hard, it sped straight for the narrow neck of the green. When it finally hit, it bounced long, then bounced again, then rolled and rolled and rolled. We could hear shouts and cheers from the distant green. Ken Venturi listened intently to his earphone for a moment.

"He's on the front edge of the green, 80 feet from the hole," he said. And Hubie Green fainted again.

But the crafty Hagen shook his head in disbelief .

"It was a lucky shot," he confided to me. "The ball must have bounced on a rock."

Then he put both hands on my shoulders and looked me straight in the eye in sincere, man-to-man fashion.

"I honestly hope you won't try a crazy shot like that and spoil your fine drive," he said earnestly. "That green is just too damned narrow to hit with a wood from this distance."

"You're absolutely right," I said, smiling to myself at the gleam of triumph that came into his eye.

I pulled out my 1-iron, hooded the blade ever so slightly and laid the ball stiff to the pin.

Hagen's jaw dropped.

"Try not to worry about your putt, Walter," I said as we started the long walk to the green. "Even with that nearly invisible hogback to putt along you won't have any trouble making par. And who knows? You might even luck in with two putts for birdie."

But he had stopped to smell some flowers and didn't seem to hear.

Hagen's approach putt was very tentative. Perhaps he was bothered by the nonexistent hogback and forgot to hit the ball. But he dropped his second for a fine birdie. A losing birdie, to be sure, but a commendable effort nevertheless. I stroked my own eagle putt firmly into the hole and started off for the 13th tee.

As I left the green, a small, intriguingly proportioned figure came out of the crowd and undulated toward me. It was Marlene Hagge, my next opponent.

I had selected Marlene Hagge because she is so gorgeous, naturally. And by watching a long series of old David Niven movies I had perfected a suave, man-of-the-world air I was certain would impress her.

But there is a world of difference between planning to sweep somebody like Marlene Hagge off her feet while she is at a safe distance and coping with an actual Marlene Hagge standing right there swishing her eyelashes at you. I was in no way prepared for that kind of voltage.

She showed no mercy.

"Would you mind terribly," she asked demurely, "if we walked to the next tee—together? I've been so hoping to get to know you better."

"Uh, yeah, I guess so, sure," I said. "OK."

Not vintage David Niven, perhaps, but it touched off a smile that melted all the electrical connections on the nearby power lawnmower.

"That's very sweet of you," she murmured, shyly taking my arm for protection against the throng.

"My! You're so strong!" she whispered. "Why, I'll have a hard time reaching this hole with a driver, but a man with muscles like yours probably won't need more than a 3-iron, or maybe even a 4!"

"Uh, yeah, I guess so," I said. "That sounds about right."

"Move your weight forward."

The 13th is a brutal par 3 of 212 yards, uphill and into a stiff wind, with the pin just a few feet from the back edge. I had planned to take a 3-wood and hit it as hard as I could.

But by the time we reached the tee I was convinced that for a man with my exciting animal magnetism, entering the glorious prime of life, with sexy gray hair and sinews of well-nigh frightening power, a 5-iron would be more than enough.

On the tee I gestured for Marlene ("Do call me Marlene. Last names are so, well, so impersonal.") to hit first.

But she explained that since I had played the last hole so magnificently, I must take the honor.

"You mustn't give me any special consideration," she said softly, "just because you may possibly have noticed that I am a woman." At the same time, my gallantry was rewarded with another incandescent smile. This one jolted me from a 5-iron down to a 6.

I strode to the tee, my enormous muscles gleaming in the sunlight.

I glanced at Marlene.

"Smite it for me!" her eyes seemed to implore.

I switched to a 7-iron and vowed to do just that.

Halfway through the smite, though, I suddenly realized that I was trying to hit a short iron nearly twice as far as it was likely to go. I made a frantic, last-second lunge with my right shoulder, pulled the ball into a tree beside the tee and watched, hypnotized, as it rattled around in the branches and finally dribbled into a bunker beside the previous green, not 50 yards away.

Marlene took her driver and whipped out a beautiful low, drawing shot that stayed well under the wind. The ball bounced on the hard apron in front of the green and rolled almost to the flagstick.

I bumbled off to my bunker, still not quite sure what I was doing there. Left momentarily to my own devices, however, I engineered a spectacular, Hagenesque recovery to less than six feet.

As I neared the green Marlene rushed out to congratulate me. Eyes shining with admiration, she begged me to show her exactly how I had hit the shot.

"Uh, yeah, sure," I said. "Um, OK."

But no matter how many times I demonstrated, she seemed unable to understand the subtleties of the grip.

"Would you mind terribly," she asked finally, blushing, "standing behind me and placing my hands on the club exactly the way you put yours?"

By the time she was completely satisfied with her grip I was lucky to get down in three putts. She made birdie.

Somewhere on the outskirts of my mind a vague theory was beginning to form. Could I have a female Walter Hagen on my hands? But before we reached the next tee I was deeply ashamed of my suspicions.

Marlene drew me aside for a moment. She was visibly upset, and her hand rested impulsively on my arm as she spoke.

"I feel just terrible about your taking a 5 on that hole," she whispered, so softly that I was forced to bend my head very close to hers in order to hear. I learned later than her perfume is a brand called "Bonecrusher," which may be sold only by special permit in most states.

"I'm afraid it may have been partly my fault," she confessed. "I was so selfish, bothering you with my silly questions."

Suddenly she looked up and blinked her eyes rapidly, struggling to keep back the tears. Unusually large eyes, I noticed, and very, very blue. Perhaps azure would be a more accurate word than merely blue. The azure of clear Mediterranean skies?

At any rate, I realized guiltily, by no stretch of the imagination could these be the eyes of a Walter Hagen.

"And now," she finished brokenly, "you probably h-h-hate me!"

Suffice it to say that on that hole I had to chip in from 30 yards to salvage a 7, which was three over par. Marlene made 4, shook hands briskly and went off to see whether Walter Hagen had any orchids left.

Lee Trevino, my next opponent, was wearing a wide grin when I tottered up to the 15th tee.

"How'd you come out with Marlene, pardner?" he inquired. "Manage to make bogey, at least?"

I shook my head, partly in answer to his question and partly in an effort to stop the faint buzzing that persisted in my ears.

He nodded sympathetically.

"That's why we don't let them on the tour with us," he confided. "Can you imagine trying to sink a downhill putt right after Laura Baugh had asked permission to feel your biceps and then said 'Ooh'?"

"Ooh?" I echoed, aghast.

"Ooh," he repeated grimly, then grunted with effort as he sent a long, low fade 270 yards down the left side of the fairway, precisely where he wanted it to go.

The 15th is a 417-yard par 4 with a slight dogleg right and sort of a mini-swamp crossing the fairway about 300 yards out. The hole was cut behind a deep, right-hand bunker, so any drive in the right half of the fairway would leave a blind approach and practically no green at all to work with.

Normally, I easily could have carried the swamp with my driver. But Marlene had taken a lot out of me. Besides, the net was beginning to fray a bit from the tremendous spin I had been putting on everybody's shots.

So I contented myself with dropping a 4-wood a few feet past

Lee Trevino's drive. I wanted him to be away, because I was sure if I hit first he'd manage to get inside me one way or another.

Lee was in high spirits, laughing and chattering away and joking with the gallery. I was grateful for the chance to relax after being drawn and quartered on the previous two holes.

But I was careful not to lower my guard completely. I knew that Trevino, for all his good cheer and sympathy, would bear watching.

He played it straight until after he hit his approach, a crisp 7-iron that went straight at the flag, bit and drew back to about 14 feet below the hole.

Then he made his move. While I was momentarily occupied with selecting my own club, Trevino winked at the gallery, then casually reached down and unzippered a large compartment on the side of his bag.

A huge rubber snake launched itself from the opening and hurtled through the air, directly at my head.

Even though I had anticipated something of the sort, I was startled by the suddenness of the attack. My head jerked back involuntarily.

But I had prepared well. Even as my head flew back, my hand flashed to a hidden remote-control button on my belt.

And as Lee Trevino rolled on the ground, convulsed with laughter over his snake trick, an 18-foot battery-operated rubber crocodile lumbered out from behind a pile of old snow tires, seized him by the leg and dragged him off under the net and into the swamp.

We all had a good chuckle while we waited for Lee to come back.

But he never did, and after waiting the full five minutes allowed under the rules, I reluctantly declared him a lost player.

We quickly discovered that Lee Trevino's thoughtless behavior had left us with a perplexing technical problem.

He had already hit his approach, so Joseph C. Dey ruled that it was only fair for me to go ahead and hit mine. I lofted a soft 8-iron that was actually a few feet too long, but got tangled in the flag and dropped in for a lucky eagle. No problem there.

Nor was the matter of a substitute player any real trouble, since I had the foresight to bring along a spare. Ken Waterman, a gentleman I used to play with in my pre-perfection days, was pressed into service. After an hour's hard work by the makeup crew Ken was deemed presentable enough.

So far, so good. But scarcely had I hoisted Ken into the air, intending to drop him over my shoulder within two club-lengths of the ball but no closer to the hole, when Joseph C. Dey raised a forbidding hand.

"Hold everything!" he said. "Seems to me there ought to be a penalty in here somewhere."

I was puzzled.

"I don't think so, Joseph C.," I said. "The rule, as I recall it, is perfectly clear: "Whosoever shall be draggeth off into ye swampe, yea and a substitute player shall forthwith be dropped and penalty shalt there be none!' "

True, if I were to drop Ken sideways part of him would come down less than two club-lengths from the hole. But I planned to drop him headfirst and repair the green when nobody was looking.

Joseph C. Dey was not convinced.

"No," he said, "I'm pretty sure there's more to that rule. Something about 'hoofed or burrowing animals,' I think. Maybe the rule is that if you're carried off by a hoofed or burrowing animal you get a free drop, but for other animals it's a one-stroke penalty. Or maybe it's two strokes."

He frowned and scratched his head. "Of course it could be the other way around," he admitted. "It's been quite a while now since I actually sat down and read the Rules of Golf, word for word."

He scratched his head again. "I'm not even sure which kind of animal a crocodile is. Or isn't. And do you suppose rubber ones count the same as real ones?"

I must confess to being a trifle miffed with Joseph C. Dey Jr. at this point. After all, he had been brought along for the express purpose of resolving the kind of predicament we were in.

Besides, my arms were beginning to get tired from holding Ken up in the air during what had turned out to be a fairly lengthy conversation.

But then Joseph C. Dey tossed back his head with the famous boyish smile that makes you love the man in spite of his short-comings.

"Oh, bother it all anyway," he said. "Penalty shalt there be none this time, but try not to make a habit of it. Play ball!"

Whereupon I dropped Ken, who lined up Lee Trevino's putt with great care and pulled it a good two feet left of the hole.

The 16th is a mere 452 yards, but it doglegs far to the left and requires a really strong drive to reach the corner. On the right is more crocodile country. On the left, deep woods.

Ken was visibly nervous on the tee, although I did my best to calm him.

"Forget that you're on national television, Ken," I said soothingly. "Forget that it's in color, with millions of people watching your every move. Never mind that your fly is open."

He nodded gratefully. But then, after watching me cut the corner with a towering 300-yard smash which left me no more than an easy 6-iron to the green, he pulled me aside.

"It's not the TV," he whispered hoarsely. "It's the distance. How can I possibly hit far enough to reach this hole in two shots?"

He looked at me appealingly.

"Surely you realize, Ken," I said gently, "that the rules forbid my assisting you, desperate though your plight may be?"

He hung his head.

"But perhaps," I smiled, "you would be interested in a question once put to me by a famous pro, before I got my net and no longer needed his expensive advice?"

Tears of hope streamed down his weather-beaten face.

"Here is the question, Ken: When you set up to the ball, are your hands fastened to your arms?"

He stopped crying.

"Do I get to know the context in which that question was asked?"

"No," I said.

Ken thought very hard. Then he squared his shoulders, strode confidently to the tee and hit the greatest drive of his life, 175 yards straight into the woods.

Sometime later he showed up on the green, where he claimed to be laying 5.

I had run into a spot of trouble myself, having hit my drive so hard that the ball was pretty well squashed. My crisp 6-iron wobbled strangely in the air, oozed down and expired in some high grass five yards left of the green and 60 feet from the hole.

Ken inadvertently stepped on the ball, which didn't help the lie. And the Winged Foot management, panicky over the way I was humbling their course, had recut the pin into the steepest slope they could find.

Under the circumstances, I think holing that particular shot for birdie required as fine a mental effort as I had made all day.

Ken three-putted, scribbled a 6 on his card and hurried off to practice his new power swing.

I approached the 17th tee with a sense of mounting excitement.

From the start, I had more or less expected that the closing holes would provide a really dramatic finish. The kind of heroics that would leave the TV people lusting for more. (I even had a title in mind for the sequel: Dream Round II.)

To this end I had reserved as my final opponent none other than Jack, the mighty Nicklaus!

But to my considerable chagrin, neither the 17th nor 18th turned out to be very exciting.

On 17 we both drove the fairway and both hit the green, Jack with a 4-wood and I with a 3-iron. I made my putt and Jack missed his. Big deal.

Play on 18 was only marginally more interesting.

We both drove the fairway again but this time Jack really boomed one. He was a good five yards past me.

Jack walked up to his ball and pulled out a 2-iron.

Then he fell over sideways.

Just like that. Plop. One minute he was pulling a 2-iron out of his bag and the next minute he was lying flat on his back on the

160

garage floor. Like a 185-pound beetle, only with not as many legs waving in the air.

I put the club back in his bag and he scrambled to his feet, looking confused.

"Damndest thing I ever saw," he told me. "David Graham made me these special irons a while ago for my birthday. Every time I lay hands on one of them I get all weak and wobbly and I fall over. Generally, I fall sideways with the long irons, forward with the medium and short irons and backwards with the wedge."

He tested the wind and took a practice swing.

"Beautiful set of irons," he said. "And David went to a lot of trouble finding some kind of special metal for the heads."

He set up to the ball and went into his patented pre-shot coma. He then shook his head and backed away.

"Still," he said, "special metal or not, it keeps on happening. I grab one of those damned irons and I suddenly get weak and I fall over."

He cut a lovely, soft 4-wood into the wind and sighed as it trickled off the back edge. Then he turned to me, the famous face a study in frustration and despair.

"Do you suppose there could be something about that metal?" he asked. "Just what the hell is kryptonite, anyhow?"

Jack finally got down in five, which was quite commendable under the circumstances. But since I had been lying two feet away for an easy birdie all the time, the finish wasn't really what you could call spine-tingling.

Even so, I was pleased with the round. Tired but happy, I transposed the garage back into the garage and headed in for supper.

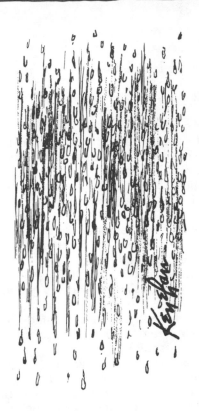

"Well, at least the weather's good."

"I attribute my win to concentration, practice, minute attention to
basic details and a dogmatic refusal to yield to pressure . . .
of course, using my lucky blue plastic tee didn't hurt any."

"That's the best shot of the day. You're
over by the entrance to the bar."

GOLF'S FLUKIEST SHOT

by HENRY LONGHURST

I long ago reached the conclusion that a hole-in-one is no more than a colossal fluke and that golfing skills play no part whatsoever in the matter. So far as I know, no one has ever been skillful enough to make a hole-in-one on purpose.

Automobiles are habitually exhibited at short holes at tournaments for the first man or woman to ace the hole, but for the most part they are still sitting there unclaimed at the end, despite the best players in the world peppering the flag for three or four days.

Just occasionally someone wins the car, but who shall say that he did it on purpose—as a result of skill superior to that of all the others? Of all the shots played to that hole, why was his the one which happened to go in?

Harry Vardon, who stood out in his day as surely as Jones, Hogan, Palmer and Nicklaus have stood out in theirs, was reputedly so accurate that the only hazards facing him in the afternoon were his own divot marks of the morning. Yet the record books credit him with only one hole-in-one. The same is said of Walter Hagen, who was no mean performer, either. Yet Art Wall is credited with 40 over the past 40 years.

Some years ago Harold Henning, one of the South African brothers, holed out in a British tournament at a hole endowed with £10,000, a tidy sum equivalent in those days to about $30,000. My first thought, somewhat unworthily, was not to congratulate him but to wonder how much they would get off him in taxes. (You think your U.S. taxes are high? You ought to try ours!)

It occurred to me at once that, if it happened to me, I should take the matter to court and claim that a hole-in-one was not a matter of skill, since no golfer in recorded history had ever made one on purpose, but rather an act of God—or, if you like, the result of a lottery or game of chance, and therefore not taxable. I am still wondering how I should have got on.

One could have brought much evidence to support the "game of chance" theory, for it seems to me that almost as many holes-

164

in-one are made with bad shots as with good. Many are the half-topped tee shots that have scuttled into the hole. Others have gone in off walls, off cottage rooms, off rocks far out-of-bounds, off wire fencing around the green, off almost anything.

An English professional playing a 303-yard dogleg hole at Nottingham hit his ball to the green, on which one of the players in front was putting. This player's putt was already in motion when the pro's ball struck it—and caromed into the hole for a 1.

And what about Jim Hadderer, a lad of 16, from Elgin, Ill., who, after having watched Paul Hahn play a trick shot while kneeling, thought he would try the same? The lad scored a hole-in-one from 190 yards. That was some time ago. I wonder if he ever made one standing on his two feet?

Another American stalwart, Mr. R. W. Bridges of the Woodlawn (Mo.) C.C., bet that he could hit a ball 150 yards with his putter. He hit it from the tee at a 196-yard hole—and holed out—presumably the longest putt ever holed in golf.

And what about Mr. Dick Colbus, from Oakland, Calif., who in an invitational tournament won an $18,500 Rolls-Royce by acing a 105-yard hole? Under the new rules he would not be allowed to take it, though for myself I cannot help feeling that I would cheerfully sacrifice my amateur status for an $18,500 automobile.

For many years I had in my own modest way claimed to hold a world record, in being the only man to have holed out twice running with the same club without putting it back in the bag. Centuries ago, when I was young, I had holed out from about 80 yards for an eagle 3 at a par-5 hole, the club being what was then known as a mashie, about a 5-iron. Without putting it back in the bag I then scored my first hole-in-one.

So profound was the effect this had on me that, when I took the same club for my second shot at the following hole, I actually thought it would go in the cup. I knew I should think it strange later on, but that is what I honestly thought at the time. I need hardly say that it didn't.

Interestingly enough, Claude Harmon made successive holes-in-one in the par-3 tournament which precedes the Masters, and he may well have made them with the same club without putting it back in the bag. However, as the holes were only 80 to 100 yards, I do not think they should count. My world record still stands.

"The tournament's 14th hole is a tough par 3 with the green guarded by traps, a small pond and, as I'm sure you can see, this cockroach right here."

PLAYING DYKER BEACH WITH LAVERNE AND SHIRLEY

by LARRY SHEEHAN

At Dyker Beach, Brooklyn's gift to golf, it is a perfect day for waiting. Hot and clear, no mosquitoes, a package of new balls in hand and a fresh breeze coming in off the Verrazzano Narrows.

The faintly salty air is the only thing links-like about this busy and storied public course which I have come to play for the first time. Dyker Beach Golf Club is, in fact, removed from the Atlantic beachfront by several city blocks and a six-lane highway. Carved out of crop lands and grazing areas 40 years ago, its character remains distinctly rural. The large number and variety of trees make the place thoroughly sylvan. The elegant bridge spanning the Narrows, which can be seen from many parts of the course, is more like a postcard in the sky than a reminder of the ocean.

The usual waiting time here is two hours on weekdays, three hours or more on weekends. When I show up this particular Thursday morning, curious about the course's reputation as a hot-bed of freewheeling hustlers and fabulous shotmaking shenanigans, the waiting time is only an hour and 45 minutes. At least, that's what it says on the sign at the counter where you pay the green fee—$3.50 on weekdays, $5.50 on weekends, special discount for senior citizens.

The municipal employee behind the counter, a white-haired woman dressed in a butcher's apron, tells me that the waiting indicator with its movable numbers goes up to 5 hours 45 minutes, but it's never been set that high. She issues me my starting ticket, a small white receipt with No. 91 faintly printed on it.

I am the 91st golfer to show up to play. It is 7 a.m.

The starting area is in a grove of tall trees full of birds and squirrels. There are two rows of green benches in front of a large blackboard. A green metal warming shed is off to one side. There's a pile of coal next to it, for the stove inside on winter days.

Beyond all this is the first hole, glittering in dawn's early light, straight and generously wide, like most of the holes at Dyker Beach, which on the scorecard is a par-70, 6,300-yard layout, though it plays much shorter if you hit them halfway straight. The one foursome I watch tee off fails to do this.

Atop the blackboard is the warning: BRIBERY IS A STATE CRIME. On the board are the digits, dots and dashes that control everybody's starting times. Show your ticket to the starter and he puts a check mark next to your number on the board. If you're in a group of friends of two, three or four, which is the way most players do it, he'll arrange to send you off that way. If you're alone, he'll stick you in space available. If you report in with your No. 91 and politely ask him (as I do this morning), "Where do I stand?" he will tell you, "On the ground, man."

I decide to stand on the ground nearby for a little while.

One of the green benches is taken up by a man stretched out and snoring peacefully, a copy of the Daily News covering his face. I scan the headlines. The other benches are half-filled. I eavesdrop. The golfers chatter idly of firemen's pensions, diets, the price of coffee and Medicare. One man, wearing orthopedic sneakers and a dish towel tucked in his belt, is describing his round of 79 yesterday to a neighbor who has a disbelieving smirk on his face.

On another bench, two youngsters in Mets T-shirts are counting their change to see how many bottles of soda they can afford to drink before their round. Behind them, four older boys are making suggestive remarks among themselves about the numerous women golfers on the grounds. No harm done, though— they talk in such a hasty street mumble that no one can understand what they're saying.

I explore the clubhouse area and discover that other waiting golfers kill time by playing chess on the broad flagstone terrace, or puttering around the bumpy practice green, or gathering in the snack bar, a dimly lit, high-ceilinged place with rickety tables and faded travel posters on the walls. It gives you the overall feeling of an intimate European railway cafe. A nice place to read the Daily News before taking a nap under it. Beverages are served in a variety of paper cups, collected from overstocked or defunct food-service operations elsewhere. I take this to be part of New York City's continuing economy campaign. I have my first coffee this morning in a "Burger King" cup from somewhere in Pennsylvania and my second one in an "Eckerd's Drug Store" cup from parts unknown.

One could squeeze in a lesson from Tommy Strafaci instead of just hanging around. Strafaci, I learn, is a gruff but highly effective instructor who loves the challenge of a lousy golf swing and has a large loyal following of both low-handicap players and wretched hackers. He has taught here 24 years and holds the course record—a 63 shot in 1965.

The way most regulars at Dyker Beach use up the hour or more between sign-up and tee-off time, I finally realize, is to disappear— go back home, run errands, do the shopping, make early Mass if it happens to be Sunday.

That is why, this day, my eventual playing partner Tom is nowhere in sight before the starter yells, "91! 92! 93! 94!" When he does show up, Tom is rubbing his jaw.

Even before we introduce ourselves he explains that, after checking in for a starting time, he made a quick trip to his dentist and had two teeth pulled. "Get things done instead of wasting time," he says.

Then he introduces himself as Tom. "It's first names only here," says he, a wiry nervous old Irishman with six clubs in his bag.

Meanwhile, the rest of our foursome—two women— materialize at the last minute. Between them the women have seven clubs. I realize I have more clubs than all of my partners combined and feel uncommonly affluent.

The women are housewives who live a stone's throw from Dyker. They remind me of TV's Laverne and Shirley.

The big-shouldered dark blonde with gypsy-like eyes is Laverne. "We are out here strictly for the fun and the sun," she declares at the outset. She is wearing high platform shoes that will force her to play all her shots today from an extreme downhill lie.

The other one is shorter and rounder and the more sensible of the two. She's wearing sandals. She plays the Shirley to her friend's slightly daft Laverne act.

I might point out here that my own ragtag golf game happens to thrive in new settings among strangers. The job of dealing with unknown quantities makes me more detached from my game, freer to perform with proper rhythm and concentration. I may not score much better than normal (in the 90's if I am lucky) but I hit more zingers and sink more putts.

The first hole sets the pattern for our round. They make me go first because I have the most clubs. I produce a fair-to-middling drive right center in the fairway, and Laverne says, "Jeez, a pro!"

Laverne herself breaks a couple of tees trying to get them into the teeing ground. Then she grabs her 3-wood in a split-hand grip and hits a looper down the middle a good 100 yards. She and Shirley shriek.

Shirley has trouble with her stance. She circles her ball for the longest time. Unsure where she belongs in relation to the target, she wiggles her feet along a semicircular path until something tells her to go ahead and hit. This process takes a full minute each time she plays a shot.

She has a nice, full backswing. Her tee shot floats left 25 yards and rattles among some trees.

Tom has exhausted himself with practice swings by now. When he gets up on the tee, he hits a ground ball to first base, then moves out smartly behind his shot.

It is 9 a.m. We are on our way!

The course itself is fun to play. Most of the holes are straight but there's enough roll and pitch in the terrain to prevent monotony. The watered fairways remain mostly green even through a fairly dry summer. The variegated trees line practically every fairway, giving a straight driver a big advantage. As most of the holes are easily reachable in regulation, the real scoring has to come on the small, well-contoured greens. Normally these putt fast and true (I have been told) but this day they putt like an Oriental rug.

Speaking of the greens, vandals steal, bend or mutilate real pins whenever they're installed, so the greenkeeper at Dyker Beach has had to resort to using makeshift sticks to mark the cups. If you're used to sighting your approach shots on a flag fluttering against the blue sky, forget it.

The offshore wind can be a factor on some holes. The day we played the breeze was in our face on the 428-yard, par-4 fourth, a scenic straightaway hole which heads for the bridge, so it played more like a par 5. By contrast, the wind was at our back on the 488-yard, par-5 seventh, so this hole, even though it is the No. 1 handicap hole on the card, actually played more like a par 4.

There are only two real doglegs on the course—the 338-yard third and the 369-yard 12th—but they are good ones, impossible to reach in less than two unless you are a big hitter like one of Dyker's legends, a guy named Boswell whom they still talk about around the course. Nobody seems to remember his first name, but he was a black dude who could airmail both those doglegs off the tee.

Another prodigious shotmaker was Arthur Potter. He used to bet unsuspecting playing partners he could hit the face of the clock tower on a school campus adjacent to the front nine at Dyker. It would take a 2-iron shot that is still on the rise 175 yards out, over the fence and through some trees, to accomplish the feat, but he would always collect.

Boswell and Potter belong to the era when Dyker Beach was one of the most competitive and action-oriented spots for golf in the whole Northeast. In the 1930's and 1940's, literally scores of scratch amateurs played regularly all year long. You had to shoot in the 60's to win the club championship.

Celebrity play added more glamour. Bandleader Paul Whiteman sometimes came to Dyker directly from concerts in his tuxedo to wait in the wee hours for a starting time. Leo Durocher, Eddie Stanky, Gil Hodges and Pee Wee Reese showed up on their off-days or after baseball season was over.

But that was back when there was still an Ebbets Field. The Dodgers long since have moved to California. The hustlers have married rich widows and retired to Florida. Dyker's glamour days are finished. At Dyker Beach today, it's the era of Laverne and Shirley, Tom and me.

Laverne has a tendency to play my ball—one of my new

Tommy Strafaci 6's—whenever hers can't be found. She does this to me on the third and sixth holes. I don't think she realizes the error even though her own balls are all quite distinctive, one being painted with an orange ring, and another bearing the imprint, "DAIRY QUEEN." I drop new balls on these two occasions rather than spoil Laverne's pleasure of being out from under trees for a change.

Shirley is seldom on the "runway," as she calls the fairway, but she has a good swing and chubby arms with power to spare. If only she could get that stance worked out. It opens and closes like an accordion. The sandals don't help.

Tom is silent. The truth is, Tom is profoundly annoyed. He does not enjoy such adventures in human relations. He doesn't like to get questions from Laverne and Shirley in the middle of his back-swing, like, "Which way do we go?" or, "Where's a water fountain?"

Laverne is the thirsty one. She keeps us up to date on the ever-changing focus of her thirst. On the third hole she desperately wants a drink of water. By the fifth hole she needs "a nice cold brew." By the time we are walking down the ninth she says she requires a martini.

And then it's all over. We are off the ninth green, back near the starter's area, when suddenly they all quit on me. It is nearly noon.

"The novocaine's wearing off," Tom declares. "No way I can play the back nine today!"

"Neither can we," says Laverne. She explains she has to get home to make lunch for her husband. "He doesn't know I play golf," she says.

"Neither did I," says Shirley.

"As you know, this year we lowered the qualifying age to 12. . . ."

"Way to go, Nicklaus. I'd break par, too, if I could bounce my ball off somebody's head onto the green."

"You might consider stiffer shafts."

A SHORT HISTORY OF LEGALIZED GOLF GAMBLING

by PETER DOBEREINER

We were at Sunningdale, near London, for the pretentiously named European Women's Open and, it being a Wednesday, my faculties were just ticking at idling speed. We Sunday paper writers tend to work up slowly toward Saturday's red alert and so the question from an American journalist rather caught me off balance.

He greeted me with an effusive "Hi!" Even making due allowances for the ebullience of American social exchanges his greeting seemed a trifle too warm and urgent. I was seized by a panicky suspicion that he was going to try to borrow money. The reality proved odder than that. "Where can I get a bed?" A bed? Did he want to buy a Georgian four-poster? Or had a chance encounter outside the locker room (remember, this was a women's tournament) produced a magical moment of instant rapport which only the immediate acquisition of a bed could consummate?

"Ah, yes, a bed" I answered lightly, as if such a request were a matter of everyday occurrence. "Well, there are beds and beds," I said, fighting for time in the hope of some hint of enlightenment. It duly came.

"And what are the odds?" he asked. My old friend did not want a bed so much as a bet. Once again the nuances of the North Carolina dialect had deceived my ear. Much the same thing happened some years previously at St. Andrews when Miller Barber accosted me in the middle of his round and asked if I knew of a restaurant. On that occasion I had launched into a eulogy about a little fish and chip shop in Anstruther when I noticed his face was registering a series of expressions which would have done credit to a student of Stanislavsky. Hatred, contempt, frustration. . . . It was his mime of hopping about on one foot which gave me the breakthrough. He wanted a rest room. It was a relief for both of us to sort out that semantic puzzle.

And now it was this beds-bets situation. In an attempt to avoid further confusion I resorted to my meager knowledge of the American tongue. "There is no need to go to a bedding sharp. You-all can put on a bed right here in the press tent."

I turned to the representative of the bookmaking syndicate who was lounging about picking his teeth and asked, "Are you laying Sandra Haynie?" He switched his toothpick to the other corner of his mouth (Humphrey Bogart fantasies are still strong in British gambling circles) and grunted, "Seven to two."

After a brief consultation with my colleague and a glance at the list of prices, I again approached the bookie with the instructions: "A handful on Rankin's nose at twelves." He nodded. "You're on." A five-pound note changed hands and three days later my friend duly collected 150 tax-free and perfectly legal dollars, thanks to the tidy short game of Mrs. Judy Rankin.

The incident illustrates one reason—perhaps the only reason— why Americans like to come to British golf tournaments. Mankind possesses an atavistic and universal urge to skin a bookie and this you can do (or attempt) with no more fuss than buying a warm beer.

That is one difference between our countries. To judge by Hollywood B-movies, America is gambling mad. Experience suggests there must be some substance in that view. Every time I visit America to cover a golf tournament, the papers are full of interviews with Jimmy (The Greek) Snyder saying that Jack Nicklaus is a 13 to 5 shot for the Masters. You can tell from the generosity of his odds that this Jimmy is prepared to put his money where his mouth is. But how, tell me, how do you get your money on? I have a sneaking feeling that the League of Purity has infiltrated the Mafia. Everyone talks about gambling, but when you get right down to it nobody outside of Nevada, or the race tracks, or a few off-track betting establishments can actually make a lawful bet.

In Britain the situation is quite different. There is a betting shop on every street corner, as dull and respectable as a bank. If the effort of walking a hundred yards is too much for you, there is always the telephone.

Remember how Doug Sanders missed a short putt which cost him the British Open at St. Andrews in 1970? In the deluge of sympathy which engulfed him on that occasion there was one message which acted like a healing balm on his disappointment. It was a check, a large check, from a bookmaker. Sanders had to prequalify for the Open that year and had been quoted at 33 to 1. He had a bundle on himself to finish in the first three.

Lee Trevino is another golfer who has been known to fatten the prize-fund kitty with a little judicious speculation. One notable member of the Royal and Ancient Golf Club is today driving around in a large and expensive Mercedes as the result of backing a long-shot winner at one tournament.

The tradition of golf gambling is as old as the game itself. The earliest records of the original Scottish clubs are devoted almost entirely to wagers. A member was elected as Recorder of the Bets and it was his job to stay reasonably sober during club dinners and to take note of the challenges thrown out by members, often blind drunk at the time, and enter them in the Bet Book.

During one of their gargantuan weekly dinners—at which, according to the historian Tobias Smollett, no self-respecting member would consume less than a gallon of claret—the members of the Honourable Company of Edinburgh Golfers fell into an argument which resulted in the following entry in the Bet Book: "Mr. R. Allan bets one guinea that he will drive a ball from the Castle Hill without the gate of the palisade into the Half-Moon battery over the parapet wall." He won, so it is recorded.

The book of the Royal and Ancient at St. Andrews has an entry which states that Sir David Moncrieffe backs his life against that of Mr. John Whyte Melville, the survivor to present a new silver cup to the St. Andrews Golf Club. Some avid historians have tried to suggest that this referred to a golf match, with the loser obliged to do the gentlemanly thing afterward and commit suicide by impaling himself on his putter. Alas for fancy. It merely meant a wager on which of them would live longer.

Long before the rise of tournament golf, professionals played challenge matches for substantial wagers. Willie Park of Mussel-burgh maintained a standing advertisement in a 19th-century golf magazine challenging all comers for a hundred pounds a side. Galleries backed their favorites and it was common for a wild drive to be kicked back onto the fairway.

Since gambling on golf has a long and slightly respectable history, it was no surprise when a large bookmaking syndicate tried the experiment recently of pitching a betting tent at a tournament. The bookies chose a small regional event, the Midlands match-play championship, for their first venture.

The qualifying rounds were at stroke play and odds were offered on the chances of each golfer beating the score of his playing partner. Now the form among the competitors was pretty well established and it did not take much prescience to see that David Snell, an experienced tournament specialist, had it all over his partner, a young assistant. One of the competitors saw his chance. He backed himself to beat his man, and doubled the bet with a win for Snell. For an outlay of 10 pounds he stood to collect 500. Which he duly did.

Anyway, the bookies were sufficiently encouraged to repeat the experiment on a larger scale. They set up shop at the John Player Classic at Turnberry, where the invited field included some illustrious visiting golfers such as Arnold Palmer, Billy Casper, Doug Sanders, Gay Brewer and Gary Player.

At times you couldn't get into that tent for the crush of caddies wagering their beer money. One enterprising group of sportsmen worked out a system of hand signals to pass information from the course back to their confederate at the betting shop. He would scan the distant sand dunes with a pair of binoculars and pick up one of his friends waving an umbrella in a pre-arranged manner, which meant that Palmer had picked up a birdie at the 10th.

Actually, waving umbrellas on golf courses can be misleading. In the not so distant past, before radio communications were commonplace, two agency reporters arranged a system to scoop the world with the first news of the winner of the British Amateur at St. George's, Sandwich. One would stand by an open telephone line at the club while the other would follow the match.

The plan was for the field man to raise his umbrella when the last putt dropped, waving it from side to side if Cyril Tolley had won and pumping it up and down in the case of a victory by Roger Wethered. The watcher from the clubhouse had his glasses on the distant sand dunes which were thronged by large crowds. He heard the burst of violent cheering which signaled the end of the match. At that moment the capricious British weather took a hand and a squall of rain swept across the links. Something like 2,000 umbrellas were raised on the instant.

"What! That can't be more than an easy 7-iron!"

HOW I CURED MY HATED SHANK

by NICK SEITZ

"Look out!" I shouted at Dow Finsterwald, it being hard to remember the standard warning of "Fore!" in a sudden crisis such as—please excuse the expression—a shank.

This was early in the week of the 1972 Phoenix Open. I had dropped by the course to pick up my press credentials and was talked into playing a practice round by Jim Hardy, a young touring pro who grew up on the same block with me in Hutchinson, Kan., and how many people can say that?

For 17 holes I played acceptably, for me. The 18th is a par 5. My second shot sank into deep rough on the right, leaving me a long wedge shot over a gaping bunker. To the right of the bunker is a practice area where Finsterwald was.

My approach shot was that unmentionable, the hated shank. It took off at right angles, straight for Finsterwald's handsome veteran head, followed closely by my stricken yelp of "Look out!" Fortunately, he saw the accursed thing coming in plenty of time to assume a prone position behind his golf bag.

"I'm very sorry," I stammered to Finsterwald 43 times, adding, "It's been years since I hit a shank."

He cringed at the infamous five-letter word. The last I saw of him he was packing up his clubs and stuffing cotton in his ears.

There are pros who have threatened bodily harm on people who mention a shank.

I know a woman, a 14-handicapper, who, instead of saying the word, spells it out as wary parents might spell out "C-A-N-D-Y" in front of a 3-year-old.

Shanking is the worst affliction in golf, compounded because if you hit one shank you are prone to hit another and then another, ad nauseam.

My near-beaning of Finsterwald, followed by other rounds marred by shanks, inspired me to learn more than I ever wanted to know about shanking.

A shank is so named because the ball is contacted on the shank part of an iron club, where the hosel meets the heel of the

177

clubhead . . . by definition you cannot shank a wood, a wood having no hosel. Another cliché about shanking is that mechanically it's the closest thing to a perfect shot, since the ball is struck very near the sweet spot on the clubface. That has to be the smallest consolation in the world.

There are, of course, several degrees of shanking. We are speaking here of the pure shank, referred to by one of my fellow editors at Golf Digest as "a bona fide lateral." He refuses to talk further about the shot, probably as a result of a recent unfortunate incident which saw him play as a guest at an exclusive private club in the area and get everyone's attention by smartly clanging a shanked iron tee shot off a nearby ball washer.

It is comforting to me to learn that some of the game's greatest players have hit some of the game's greatest shanks. My own favorite shanking story centers on Australia's talented Peter Thomson who, intending a little chip shot onto the green, one sad day shanked the ball four consecutive times, all the way around the green without touching it and back to where he had begun.

Johnny Miller shanked his way out of a victory in the Bing Crosby tournament one year. Jack Nicklaus and Gay Brewer have shanked in the courtly atmosphere of the Masters Tournament, whose immortal founder, Bobby Jones, is himself said to have fought the shanks.

Some years ago, touring pros Harry Cooper and Frank Walsh were having breakfast together on the last day of a competition in Florida. Walsh was a curious fellow, always asking questions.

"Have you ever shanked?" he wondered of Cooper.

"No, I never have," Cooper replied.

"Never?"

"No."

"Do you know how a shank happens?" persisted Walsh.

"Sure," said Cooper. "I've taught people how to stop shanking."

Later that day, Cooper needed a par 4 on the 18th to win the championship. He had an 8-iron shot to the green. Assaying the shot, he noticed Walsh standing behind the green watching the finish. Cooper recalled their breakfast conversation. He thought to himself what an awful time it would be to hit the first shank of his life. And he shanked to lose the tournament.

Not that shanking is all bad. Lee Trevino tells me a shank made him rich. He lost the 1968 Houston Champions tournament when he shanked on the last hole. Consequently, he went into the U.S. Open at Rochester that year with no big commercial deals and, when he won it, was free to negotiate lucrative endorsements. Today we see him on television a wealthy man, behind the wheel of his Dodge car in his Wrangler clothes washing down Bayer Aspirin with a bottle of Dr. Pepper.

A shank can be caused, according to Trevino and other experts on the subject who are willing to discuss it, by such phenomena as: letting your weight drift toward the ball, swinging too fast from the top, lazy hand action. There are more home remedies for shanking than for hiccups: try to hit the ball off the toe of the club; have a friend place his hand on your forehead to keep your weight back, two shots of bourbon mixed with a spoonful of warm honey and a dash of lemon juice. I tried them all.

Finally I stopped shanking. I don't know whether one of the cures worked or the devil got bored with harrassing me or the shanks just went away. I don't care—so long as they stay away.

"We lost, Charlie, because you weren't concentrating."

"Well, after 20 years of trying, say hello to the club champ, Agnes."

"File your 1040 yet?"

THE HALTER-TOP CAPITAL OF THE TOURNAMENT WORLD

by GARY CARTWRIGHT

I don't know what was going through John Schroeder's mind as 20,000 spectators watched him line up a putt worth $18,000 on the final hole of the final day of Colonial Country Club's 1977 golf tournament, but I was thinking about my old Granny. The 25-foot putt would enable Schroeder to tie for first place and force a sudden-death playoff with Ben Crenshaw. It was easily the most important putt in Schroeder's eight years on the professional tour: although Schroeder's yearly earnings have climbed as high as $67,000, he is considered an unknown.

In contrast, Crenshaw, the young Austin High and University of Texas graduate, has won more than $500,000 since turning pro in 1973 and is considered the Jack Nicklaus of his generation. I knew what my old Granny would be thinking as Schroeder drew back his putter. She would be thinking: Miss it, turkey! And so he did, by a fraction of an inch.

Granny used to think that golf was a cream-puff game, redeemed only by the fact that it occupied the weekends of men who would otherwise be foreclosing on small farms and roping widows and orphans (Granny was both) to railroad trestles. Then about 1960, television introduced her to Arnold Palmer. Palmer reminded sportswriters, and by extension my Granny, of a black-smith hammering out his trade on an anvil, and on that image the masses rose up and swallowed the game as mindlessly as they would have swallowed a new brand of shrimp-flavored almonds.

Golf had its good guys and its bad guys—Granny never cared much for Gary Player because he dressed in black and was a foreigner (from South Africa), and it took her a spell to adjust to the news that Jack Nicklaus had once been a fraternity boy at Ohio State. Golf was both childishly simple and vicariously egalitarian, so long as it was exercised, as Granny exercised it, in front of a 17-inch TV screen. It was a remarkable sight to walk into Granny's tiny living room, cluttered with yellowing photographs of catfish she had caught and relics preserved from the 1936 Texas Centennial, there to find the old lady playing out her remaining weekends perched in front of her Montgomery Ward ("Monkey Ward" she called it) black-and-white set, dipping Garrett snuff and pontificating such wisdom as, "Arnie was making a run on the field till he chili-dipped that wedge on 14."

Granny lived all of her life in or around Fort Worth but never saw a Colonial, except on TV. When I was a sportswriter, I offered to take her, but I might as well have asked her to put on her best housedress and come meet the Queen of England. "What would I do out there with all them high-muckety-mucks?" she wanted to know. Granny wasn't a social climber. Her idea of high rolling was taking a city bus to Leonard's Department Store's free parking lot, catching the private subway that connected to the store's huge basement, purchasing a spool of No. 1 thread, dining on fried perch and peach cobbler at the Leonard's cafeteria and returning home in time to watch Arnold Palmer's "Tips on Golf," which preceded the tournament of the week.

Once, when we were driving through Forest Park, I turned off impulsively on Colonial Parkway, which skirts the rosebush-laced fences of the golf course and circles in front of the country club's faintly antebellum red-brick clubhouse. "You're fixin' to get us arrested," Granny warned. I told her that Colonial Parkway was a public thoroughfare, the same as her own modest street. If that was so, she asked, then why did a high-muckety-muck like Marvin Leonard, the department store mogul and founder of Colonial, live there? I said that Marvin didn't actually live at Colonial. It was true that he had built Colonial and supervised its rebuilding after a series of fires and floods, but now he had built a second country club, Shady Oaks, and it was my understanding that he made his home somewhere in that neighborhood. Shady Oaks was now *the* club in Fort Worth. I asked if she was interested in seeing Shady Oaks, but Granny's old eyes had wandered through the stately oaks and elms and out to the perfectly manicured 17th fairway, where a group of men in Banlon shirts and straw hats were preparing to hit their drives. "It's the most beautiful thing I ever saw," she said.

As I watched John Schroeder miss the most important putt of his life, my heart sank in a small, permanent way. Granny had hexed him from the grave. Arnie and Jack weren't even in the field, but I knew Granny would already have taken Ben Crenshaw to heart with the same unwavering zeal that she felt back in the 20's the first time she watched the Fighting Texas Aggie Band parade through Fort Worth. Crenshaw had that special zing. If Palmer was a blacksmith, Crenshaw was a sculptor. Twenty thousand groaned as Schroeder missed his big putt, but later, when everyone was drunk and mellowed out on a hard week of socializing and name playing, all you heard was, "What a great finish for a great tournament!"

Poor Schroeder. I guess second place wasn't so bad, seeing as how he won $22,800 and got to appear on national TV in the shadow of Ben Crenshaw.

Poor Schroeder.

Inching along with the tournament traffic on Colonial Parkway early in May, I observed residents hawking parking spaces on their front lawns for $5. A few hundred yards from the clubhouse was a barricade guarded by a policeman who rerouted all motorists not possessing Super Saints badges. All other categories—the ordinary Angels, Patrons, club members and plain folks with $15 tickets— were directed to the TCU Stadium parking lot where buses waited to ferry them to the golf course. There are 1,600 members of Colonial and a waiting list of six months, but only a few hundred wear the gold badges of Super Saints. Aside from the color of their badges, there is one other way to recognize Super Saints. They don't sweat. It is an acquired art. For the privilege of playing in the pro-am, enjoying valet parking and gaining entrance to the exclusive Terrace Room overlooking the 17th tee and the 18th green, Super Saints purchased $1,500 worth of tickets. Mere Angels absorbed only $750 in tickets, and so on down the pecking order. In a way, the police barricade near the clubhouse represented a final bastion separating the plutocrats from the plebeians. It was somehow sad to watch an exquisitely proportioned young woman with the word "SPOILED" printed on her T-shirt being turned away.

The Terrace Room is not a good place to watch a golf tournament, but it has been my observation that Super Saints do not come to watch, but to be watched. From the ground you can look up and see them cool as cloisonné behind tinted glass. In case anyone has a passing interest in the tournament, there are TV sets strategically situated in every room of the clubhouse: the Chalet Room, the Mirador Room, the Gold Room, the Cork Room, the 19th Hole and the Men's Card Room—these being the hangouts of Angels and mortals—all of them packed with revelers, make-out artists and wool inspectors. "Wool" is a sporting-world euphemism for . . . well, for good-looking women. One former tournament chairman is known affectionately to the press as Old Wool. A Fort Worth doctor caught in the act of leering at a nifty in a thin halter told me: "It's OK. I have a clearance from my wife to leer at anything above a 36-B cup." There was an oilman who used to position himself in the 19th Hole with a prepared sign that said: TELL THE ONE IN BLUE TO TURN AROUND. Probably the most memorable scene in Colonial archives was an act of flagrante delicto near the 15th fairway, captured, quite by luck, by an ABC cameraman testing his equipment. This classic piece of photojournalism has since been shown—privately—worldwide, and the performers, who were not married to each other, are no longer married to anyone. And Cullen Davis, the multimillionaire charged with murdering his stepdaughter and his wife's lover, used to park his trailer near the clubhouse and treat his guests to private screenings of "Deep Throat."

Cullen was in the jailhouse and not available for this year's tournament, but his estranged wife, Priscilla, star witness in the murder case, was highly visible in tight white pants and a blouse that covered the scar on her stomach and very little else. Priscilla was accompanied by her bodyguard, an off-duty homicide detective, and her presence in the Terrace Room less than a year after the murder created the kind of stir you would expect on finding Truman Capote in Gloria Vanderbilt's shower. A few Super Saints openly greeted her; the rest openly snubbed her. There wasn't a trace of indifference. Tom McCann, former mayor of Fort Worth and a man who himself has known adversity, sat holding Priscilla's hand and telling her how the tournament just wasn't the same without Cullen; though of course he was delighted to see her alive and maybe when this thing was all over everyone could get together like in the good old days.

In a sense Priscilla Davis epitomized the style and spirit of Colonial. If it was true that the real pooh-bahs of Fort Worth now formed their alliances in the sedentary lounges of Shady Oaks, Colonial was still where things happened. CBS sports commentator Tom Brookshier, who has been around, observed that Colonial was "the halter-top capital of the world," and Norm Alden, a former Fort Worth disc jockey who went on to become a minor actor best known for his AAMCO commercials, noted, "If you don't like what you see at Colonial, you're too old to be looking." I don't have the figures to prove it, but I'd wager that a majority of the members at Shady Oaks hold dual memberships at Colonial, if for no other reason than to be a part of the yearly rites. One of the city's better-known gamblers was doing a few card tricks for the oilmen in the Men's Card Room, and Hayden Fry, athletic director at North Texas State, lobbied appropriate powers on behalf of his school's campaign to join the Southwest Conference. Willie Nelson was supposed to be at Colonial, but he overslept.

Back in the days of Ben Hogan the biggest celebrities you were likely to encounter inside the clubhouse were golfers, but that practice seems to have gone the way of all things. I didn't spot a single golfer in any of the hangouts, not that I would necessarily recognize one. Golfers used to have names like Hogan, Snead, Nelson, Palmer and Nicklaus—these days they are called Tewell, Cerrudo, Kratzert, Zoeller and Curl, and if that sounds like a seat on the New York Stock Exchange my point is made. Golf is the only sport I can think of where success is measured almost entirely by how many trips you make to the bank. Where once a man had to be rich to play golf, now the reverse seems true. No less than a dozen golfers currently on the tour have pocketed more than a million dollars. (There now are 15 over the million mark.) When you're playing for those kinds of stakes, who has time to sit around jabbering with local Super Saints? When you read down the list

184

of golf's top 50 all-time money winners you will not find Hogan, Middlecoff, Demaret, Nelson, Sarazen, Hagen or Armour. Slamming Sammy Snead, who has made more rounds than the sun and moon, is currently listed in 39th place; a transitory footnote when you realize his undistinguished nephew, J. C. Snead, is 24th. Young Ben Crenshaw, who first attracted attention in 1973 when, still an amateur, made a run at the Masters, has climbed into 41st position, as of this writing (1977).

Though he lives in Fort Worth, Ben Hogan no longer plays or even attends Colonial. He can't stand the crowds. During the tournament I asked a friend of Hogan's what the great man was doing with himself these days. "Practicing," the friend said. "Sometimes he'll play a few holes alone with his caddie, but his legs won't make it through 18. But there's not a day goes by you won't find him on the practice tee. If he hits 20 balls on the green, you can cover them with your coat."

In recognition of the fact that he has won the National Invitation Tournament, as Colonial is officially known, a record five times, and also because he redesigned several of the holes— supervising the removal of a number of trees including the big oak on No. 1 fairway that he used to hit regularly—Colonial is known as "Hogan's Alley." Almost all of Hogan's trophies are on permanent display in a room adjacent to Colonial's main lobby, but hardly anyone stops to look. Breaking one of my two cardinal rules for watching Colonial, I decided to visit the Hogan Trophy Room. As I stood there admiring a phonograph record with a sterling-silver label identifying it as "an address by Dr. Granville Walker (Ben's pastor) in commemoration of Ben Hogan's British Open victory, July 27, 1953," I was suddenly aware of two young girls in shorts. They were breathing on the display glass and drawing hearts in their own fog. They asked me to get them a couple of beers. "You can sign my daddy's name," one of them told me. I asked if either of them had ever seen Ben Hogan, and after some reflection one answered: "I think I used to watch it on TV."

Poor Hogan.

In the final day of the tournament I violated my second cardinal rule—I stepped outside where it's hot and where the plebeians with $15 tickets get so caught up in looking at each other's backs they are liable to trample you. Earlier, from the third-floor balcony, I had observed this seemingly endless stream of humanity that poured over the horizon like the Great Wall of China and had reflected on their motives: Perhaps they came on the off chance that they might see someone hit a golf ball. Standing now in the crush, I realized the folly of this reasoning. Nobody who is not being paid guild wages (a sportswriter, for example) should ever take it on himself to walk on a golf course. I remembered how I hated Colonial when I worked for the old Fort Worth Press, how my main job was to roam the fairways and jot down notes that

"Hey, guys! Guess who I found in the rough along 13?"

"Tempo! Tempo!"

would appear at the tail of someone else's story. I remembered how easy it was to hang close to the pressroom bar and let them come to me.

> ". . . Chi Chi Rodriguez, the fun-loving Puerto Rican, delighted the gallery when he paused beside the pond on No. 1, opened a can of beans and ate them with a spoon . . . Rumors that Bantam Ben Hogan never opens his mouth, either on or off the golf course, were put to rest today when the Wee Ice Mon turned to Porky Oliver on the 14th green and remarked, 'You're away.' "

The best place to watch Colonial was, and still is, the pressroom, located directly above the 18th green. If you stand at the window long enough, you'll see everyone worth seeing. There is a bar, a buffet, a roving waitress to take drink orders, a color TV, a giant leader board, a communications officer who knows instantly every bogey and birdie going down and enough mimeographed material to fill a garbage truck. In the old days, if you wanted to talk to a certain golfer, you had to find him yourself. Now they deliver him to the pressroom like room service. Years ago a kid named Lehmmerman drove a cab and moonlighted as a sportswriter for the Press, but someone caught him talking to Hogan and they had to let him go. Trouble was, he was talking as he marched stride for stride with Hogan down the 18th fairway in the final crucial minutes of a tournament. He was saying, "C'mon, Ben, open up. What are you really feeling inside?"

Poor Lehmmerman.

It occurred to me as I moved along at the will of the crowd that Colonial would soon have to limit attendance. Vergal Bourland, Colonial's general manager, later confirmed it. Colonial stopped estimating attendance in 1969 when its one-millionth "visitor" passed through the gates, but every year the crowds are larger. "I think we've about peaked out," Vergal told me. "I'd guess our maximum is 25 thousand daily, and we must be close to that now." Vergal noted that during the tournament there were 462 employees on the Colonial payroll, and that didn't include 250 volunteers from the membership. Of course revenue from the tournament was staggering: $450,000 in advance ticket sales plus the flood of bucks from food and drink concessions. The problem seems to be that the IRS is re-examining Colonial's status as a nonprofit organization. Where once club members tolerated the tournament, now they depend on it.

Colonial members pay the lowest dues in town, one member told me. This is consolation for the fact that it is nearly impossible to use their magnificent golf course—in order to play golf on Saturday it is mandatory that club members queue up every Wednesday at 5 p.m. and draw for starting times. I don't know if this was as Marvin Leonard intended when he opened Colonial in

1936, but given his rag-merchant proclivities, I expect it was.

Anyway, you can see why Mr. Marvin had to build himself a second country club.

Marvin Leonard is dead now, and the once great department store that he and his brother founded sits on the north edge of downtown Fort Worth boarded and abandoned like an old amusement park. During its heyday 20 or 30 years ago "Leonard Brothers' " (as Granny called it until the day she died) was the prototype of the modern shopping mall, with everything from gourmet food to overalls available under one roof. The store and its subsidiaries (one was called Everybody's Department Store) occupied several square blocks. Marvin's slogan, which appeared below the store logo, was "More merchandise for less money." Leonard's had the first escalator I ever saw, and the first subway. Mr. Marvin made his mark among retailers by purchasing enormous quantities of a single item (he once bought 50 carloads of lard from a bankrupt San Antonio grocery chain and sold it 33 cents a gallon below wholesale), using these as leads to bring people like Granny to town. Those who knew Marvin Leonard well called him the Kingfish.

"There was something magic about the Kingfish, something that inspired everyone around him," says Berl Godfrey, Colonial's first president. Berl recalled the Saturday during World War II when he and Marvin sat up all night watching the clubhouse burn down. Because of the war all building materials were restricted. While everybody else was throwing up their hands and bemoaning a duration without cocktails and grilled sirloin, the Kingfish slipped over to Stamford and purchased a condemned schoolhouse. He tore it down, shipped the best heavy timber to Colonial and sold the salvage to cover construction costs.

Berl remembered why the Kingfish built Colonial in the first place. Aside from the fact that the old dairy where it is now located and the adjacent farmland that is now Tanglewood were dirt cheap and the nearest thing to a sure bet any businessman could pray for, a country club, even if it was non-profit, could generate truckloads of profits for the man who developed the land around it. But money was only one of the Kingfish's motives. Bent-grass greens. That was his real reason. Bent grass, if you can figure out how to keep it watered and drained, stays green all year. Unable to convince the board members at Rivercrest Country Club to install bent grass, the Kingfish bought the land along the Trinity River and built his own golf club. With revenue from the slot machines that once lined its lobby, Colonial paid for itself in three years.

In 1941, five years after the club opened, the Kingfish lured the U.S. Open to Fort Worth, the first time golf's most prestigious tournament was ever played south of the Mason-Dixon line. By 1946 Colonial was a regular event on the pro golf tour, years before Houston and Dallas became tour stops. Having Ben Hogan around didn't hurt Colonial's image. Nobody said no to Hogan, except the Kingfish. When Leonard decided to build Shady Oaks as a lead item for a housing project on 1,400 acres of land he owned in Westover Hills, Hogan helped design the course; but it was the Kingfish who personally supervised the bent-grass greens.

Colonial lost something when the Kingfish died. Cecil Morgan Jr., a UT basketball player from the early 50's, son of one of Colonial's charter members and himself a current member of the club's board of governors, recalled, "My dad wouldn't let me play until I had first walked the course with Mr. Marvin and learned the ethics of the game. Don't stand behind a player who is hitting . . . don't stand on the opposite side of the cup when a player is putting . . . things people don't always teach anymore. Even after I mastered ethics, I still had to take 10 lessons from the club pro before my dad ever let me strike a ball on the course."

By Saturday afternoon John Schroeder was making a shambles of the competition and the party in the Terrace Room was beginning to look like Red Square on Lenin's birthday. Jaded and bored by what was (or was not) taking place on their golf course, Super Saints jostled for a place at the bar and waved fistfuls of dollars at immobilized waitresses. What they needed was a miracle.

The miracle's name was Ben Crenshaw.

There is some dispute whether Crenshaw won the tournament or Schroeder lost it, but it amounts to the same thing. Even when Schroeder was leading by five strokes and threatening the course record, Crenshaw was hovering over Colonial like a monster hawk. When Crenshaw's 15-foot birdie putt disappeared in the cup on 18, Schroeder's lead was reduced to a single stroke. "If I play a good solid round of golf tomorrow, Ben's just gonna have to beat me, that's all," Schroeder said later. "This course is too tough to be aggressive. I'm not gonna do anything heroic unless I have to." Schroeder told the press that when he teed it up on Sunday he wouldn't be playing Ben Crenshaw, or the course, or the crowd: He would be playing John Schroeder. Considering that Schroeder's best previous finish at Colonial was a tie for 56th place, that was a tall order.

Because the pace of the game is so agonizingly slow, a golfer's major problem is concentration. Strolling from tee to green may be exercise to your average duffer, but when you are playing for these kinds of marbles it can be like a week in the nuthouse. Even golfers who have known great success can go bonkers. Lee Trevino copes with the long anxiety between shots by pretending he is still a 10-year-old street urchin sneaking on the muny course after dark, using a broomstick wedged in a Dr. Pepper bottle for a driver. Jack Nicklaus claims that as he hits a golf shot he imagines himself hitting a perfect golf shot in a movie sequence. If Crenshaw has a secret, it is this same ability to picture perfection just before his body is required to emulate it. In his good days, Arnold Palmer used to charge the pin. It was almost like he was daring the ball to land anywhere except where he willed it. In contrast, Crenshaw seems to tiptoe toward his mark. Crenshaw grew up idolizing Palmer, but the first time they went head to head (in the 1973 Masters, when Crenshaw was still an amateur) it was like a stroll through the park. "I never thought about playing Arnold Palmer," Crenshaw told me. "I just played the course. He shot 77. I shot 73. The next day I played with Nicklaus for the first time. I had a 72. He had 77." Like many great artists, Crenshaw has reduced his philosophy to a one-liner: "Never do anything stupid."

Schroeder played his "good solid round of golf" on Sunday, but it didn't matter. Crenshaw played a little better. Schroeder started the day with a one-shot advantage, but when he faced that final putt on 18, Crenshaw had a one-shot advantage and was already in the locker room watching it on TV.

If he had hit the ball a fraction of an inch to the left, Schroeder would have forced Crenshaw into a sudden-death playoff. I'm not sure Schroeder wanted that. I know the mob in the Terrace Room didn't.

There was a time when the most important thing to remember at Colonial was your gawdam place. No more, no more. Even the Terrace Room, exclusive haunt of the Super Saints, swarmed that last night with riffraff who wouldn't know bent grass from Oaxacan blue. The exquisite young thing in the T-shirt that said "SPOILED" had finally made it inside and was drawing more attention than Priscilla Davis.

Nonmembers were filing out the gates now, happy it was over. So were the members, who drank with both hands and talked about wool, present and past. I could see Vergal Bourland chewing out a cop. Granny would have liked Vergal. Vergal knew his place. I remembered the night of the First and Last Annual Colonial Poolside Luau—mid-60's would be my guess—how Vergal or one of his lackeys forgot to invite me, and how with the help of a friend I bribed a waiter out of his uniform and headed with a tray of rolls down the long hallway toward the pool. About midway down the hall, I ran into Vergal.

"What is this?" he asked.

"Rolls," I told him.

"What for?" he asked, his voice slipping out of register.

"For hungry people," I told him.

"Is this a joke?" he said.

I told him that hunger wasn't a joke and never had been, then darted behind him and disappeared into the crowd. Although I was surely the first white waiter Colonial had ever seen, I walked past security as easily as the Kingfish selling Granny his recipe for possum and sweet taters. Hawaiian torches illuminated the freshly scrubbed club members who sat poolside, eating roast pig and

190

watching as the current Miss Universe conducted a fashion show
on the one-meter boards. I was headed for a table of friends when
a Fort Worth cop shot me the badeye. He knew what was wrong,
and as soon as he figured out what to do about it, there would be
trouble. I headed straight for the ladder to the diving platform. Miss
Universe and two models were using the low boards, so I said a
little prayer for Granny and climbed the ladder, balancing my tray
of rolls as only a man of my class could. I walked to the end of the
three-meter board, paused to enjoy the show, then jumped
spraddle-legged into a pool of floating orchids strung on wire
spokes that hurt like hell when you go crashing through them. I
ruined my wristwatch, but I got a good newspaper column out of it.
I figured Vergal would have me banned for life, but when I
referred to him in my column as "the long-suffering Vergal Bourland," he laughed. Old-timers at Colonial still talk about it.

About Vergal laughing.

Poor Vergal.

"Yes it has . . . it's been a terrible winter."

"Hey, Frank! They're OK!"

". . . Winner of the fastest round due to a
jammed accelerator on his golf car. . . ."